A CENTURY OF MODEL TRAINS

Allen Levy

Crescent Books

NEW YORK

*" The ball I threw while playing in the park
Has not yet reached the ground."* Dylan Thomas

CONTENTS

Photography   Rob Inglis
Design   John B. Cooper
Editorial Consultant   Prof. J. B. Kelly
Copyright © MCMLXXIV by A. Levy & R. Inglis
Library of Congress Catalog Card Number: 76-8378
All rights reserved.
This edition is published by Crescent Books a division of Crown Publishers, Inc.
by arrangement with New Cavendish Books.
a b c d e f g h
Phototypeset by Tradespools Ltd., Frome, Somerset.
Printed by Smeets in the Netherlands.
Bound by The Nicholstone Bookbinding Co., Nashville, USA.

ENTRE NOUS

My father's absence on service during the last war put paid to any claims I might have had to vast childhood memories of model railways. In fact, the nearest I came to owning a 'proper' locomotive was an aunt's promise in 1946 to return from a trip to London with a Bassett-Lowke 'Enterprise'. In the event, she returned with a Dinky Toy Scout Car – perhaps the price induced amnesia, or she met a salesman who had yet to find his true vocation!

Evacuation from London during the war, a first glimpse of the sea, and later, travels abroad were all experiences primarily remembered for their close links with steam powered railway journeys. Those impressions, together with the hours spent – or misspent – at various London termini watching the great expresses come and go, were enough to form the basis of a lifelong interest in railways – both prototype and make-believe.

In the early 1960's my interest in collecting model trains was confined to a few models typical of the railways I had known, but my curiosity was soon to take me down the long tunnel, away from my own nostalgia and into a world of model railways which existed long before my time or recollection.

In early 1968 I became (in retrospect quite by accident) a co-founder and for some three years a Director of Bassett-Lowke (Railways) Limited (a company formed primarily to market new lines in association with the original Bassett-Lowke company at Northampton). During that rather extraordinary departure in my career, I travelled with the company's exhibition on the famous yet commercially ill-fated Flying Scotsman Tour of the US in 1969 from Boston down to Houston ... *a folie de grandeur* on a magnificent scale. That period saw the last attempt to breathe life into the model railway department of Bassett-Lowke in so far as it concerned the Northampton factory (although industrial modelling, including railway projects, is still a major activity there). These years also saw the final production of the gauge 0 'Mogul' series which had lasted in one form or another for some 45 years.

When my commercial involvement with the company ceased, my interest in model trains was directed towards the re-establishment of my former collection, an interest spurred by my having witnessed a whole generation of buried treasure pass through Bassett-Lowke Railways' premises housed with Steam Age (a firm originally founded by Ivan Scott in association with Jonathan Minns) at Cadogan Street in London. Upon reflection, those years were to prove invaluable in the preparation of this book, for without the encouragement and assistance of the many friends which I then made all over the world, I doubt that this work would have been possible.

I hope that as a result of my collaboration with a photographer (Rob Inglis) and designer (John Cooper) of exceptional skill and feeling, the book will impart some of the joy I have experienced in discovering model trains and in tracing their development from primitive toy imagery to highly sophisticated models. The predominant use of black backgrounds in the illustrations was a conscious effort to project the image of trains emerging from other eras and being observed anew, this time, not wholly as boyhood dreams, but as sculptural objects reflecting the aesthetic values of their various times. Finally, in re-reading Alexanders' 'The Collector's Book of the Locomotive', I was grateful to be reminded that "One picture is worth ten thousand words. . . ."

Allen Levy
London

INTERNATIONAL INDEX OF MANUFACTURERS

INTRODUCTION

This book endeavours to illustrate a broad panorama of commercially produced model trains from about 1870 to the beginning of this decade. Perhaps it could more accurately have been entitled 'A Century of Model Trains – A European View'. I have tried to avoid presenting a work that purports to be all things to all men, leaving it to braver souls to tackle the subject from a totally universal standpoint.

What are commercially produced model trains? My definition would include all toy and model railway products made by individuals, firms or companies whose main livelihood is or was derived from the production of these items, or for whom their manufacture is an integral, if ancillary part, of their activities. The vast majority of items falling within this definition have, from time to time, been available at retail shops and stores. Commercially produced model trains were, of course, in being long before 1870, but it was about that time that earlier and existing trends in manufacturing converged to form what was to be the mainstream of model train production thereafter.

The majority of models illustrated in this book were produced primarily for scenic running (although not necessarily on rails or even for that matter by self propulsion). One or two locomotives illustrated may have passenger-hauling capacity, but it is not my intention to deal with the general subject of miniature passenger-hauling locomotives and stock, nor with one-off exhibition items and that whole body of work produced by the 'non-commercials'. Much discipline was needed to exclude the latter; nonetheless, one or two items have been allowed to slip through the net so as to illustrate a particular point. In view of the relative obscurity of certain manufacturers, I have tried, where possible, to include examples of their products, e.g. those of Schoenner of Germany, Stronlite of Japan and Jubb of England.

The book is arranged in six sections, four of them devoted to a general chronological review, and the remainder to specific aspects of the subject. The chronological sections have been made to correspond as far as possible with the watersheds of development over the century, although in some instances items produced in earlier periods have been transposed to later sections – in several instances the converse applies – in order to preserve a particular grouping or, to pursue (dare I say it?) a train of thought! In general, when dealing with these four sections, I have tended to follow established thinking, introducing new information only when reasonably certain of its authenticity. For the period after the second world war, a more personalised approach appeared necessary, since, like others, I ran into the problem of proximity and of trying to give shape to a period when so many models were produced out of their historical context. There was, in short, an unprecedented range of locomotives (and to a much lesser extent, rolling stock), produced, based on prototypes that were no longer contemporary. The penultimate section, 'A Glimpse of Fine Scale', illustrates the standards set by two perfectionists in their respective fine-scale 0 gauge layouts. The book concludes with a glance at the work of J S Beeson, whose locomotives, and especially the later ones, will, I believe, occupy a prominent place amongst that body of work which future critics will come to consider as representing the true *fine art* of the twentieth century.

In a work of this nature an author calls upon the experience, views and judgements of many people. In this connection I would offer my deep and special appreciation to Carole Montague for her endless attention to the text and to W. E. Finlason for his almost unique knowledge of many aspects of this subject. I would also like to thank the following for giving up their time to deal with specific points, or for supplying particular material: Matt Ascough, O. Baur, Bob Beader, Beatties, J. S. Beeson, Dr. A. Bommer, W. C. I. Brealey, Royston Carss, Carstens Publications Inc., Messrs. Clarkson of York, Count Giansanti Coluzzi, Marcel Darphin, Grafar Limited, Gebr. Fleischmann, The late David Fuest, Roland H. Fuller, L. Hertz, T. B. Hinchley, Ed. Hoffman, Laura Inglis, W. E. Jackson, Kalmbach Publishing Co., Ernst Paul Lehmann, Gebr. Märklin, Ron McCrindell, Jonathan Minns, Patrick Minns, John Proctor, Victor Reader, M. Richardson, Mel Roberts, J. Swain, Colin Sparrow, F. R. Titman, W. & H. (Models) Limited, Wilag.

AN INDUSTRY EMERGES

By 1870 a definable industry manufacturing model trains had emerged. The spectrum ranged from delicate hand-painted trains from France, principally for trackless running, all the way to ponderous, brass, live steam locomotives mainly of English manufacture. Radiguet of France also produced items of the latter type, although in a more delicate style.

The German industry supplied items which, in the main, fell between those two extremes, the vast majority of them being wholly unpretentious toys of immensely robust construction.

In the USA trains were fashioned from cast iron, tin, wood and pasteboard, and many American products of that period appeared almost prehistoric when set beside their European counterparts.

Neither toys nor models bore anything but a passing resemblance to prototype, but then novelty was all, and the brave new age of scale (and attempted scale) model trains would await the turn of the century.

1 A clockwork floor train manufactured by the firm of Mathias Hess, reputed to be one of the original toy makers of Nuremburg. This particular example has been completely restored, but fortunately the original trade mark on the smokebox front has survived.
Circa 1865 (track width 2¾").
Photo Udel Studios   E. Hoffman Collection

2 Typical of early French, hand-painted tinplate is this little 2–2–0 clockwork 'carpet toy' locomotive, accompanied by coaches bearing the destination boards '1er Class' by Dessin (DS) *circa 1880*. (Track width 2¼".) Beneath the embankment, road vehicles of the day speed by. Above, somewhat before its time, a tin aeroplane soars (borrowed from a toy roundabout).

3 A selection of English-made locomotives, all for gauge 0, reproduced from a late nineteenth-century Stevens's Model Dockyard catalogue.

2 An extremely unusual live steam floor train by Schoenner. Probably one of the few locomotives ever supplied with a single axle tender wheel arrangement. *Circa 1890*. (Track width 2½″.)
Photo Udel Studios　　　　E. Hoffman Collection

1 A superb clockwork floor locomotive by Maltète et Parent, *circa 1880*. (Track width 3⅛″.)
Photo Nauroy Studios　　　Count Giansanti Collection

3 A clockwork floor locomotive listed by Althof Bergmann and Company in 1874.

4 Another example of an early French tinplate, 'carpet toy', this time for the English market. The little clockwork 0–2–0 (track width 2″), heads coaches bearing destination boards 'London/Manchester'. Note the unusual coloured dyes applied to the wheels, typical of the work of this period by FV. *Circa 1885*. The lovely German-made bus is labelled 'The Electric Omnibus Company'.

5

5 'The Jewel in the Crown', a superb clockwork floor train, once again by Dessin, *circa 1880*. (Track width $2\frac{5}{8}''$.) While all the livery and parts are original, this train was subject to painstaking restoration, the purpose of which was to preserve the original livery intact, while preventing further flaking of the very fragile paintwork. The work was carried out by C. Littledale of Brighton, who currently ranks as one of the foremost restoration artists in the model train world today.

2 An American style, 4–2–2 steam powered floor locomotive by Schoenner, track width 3½″, *circa 1885*.
Photo Udel Studios   E. Hoffman Collection

1 An American 4–4–0 and tender in live steam for 5″ gauge, purported to be by Schoenner, *circa 1895*. (This locomotive is missing the leading pair of truck wheels.)
Photo Lewis Studios   M. Roberts Collection

3 Floor train comprising American 4–4–0 and tender, in live steam, plus car by Schoenner, *circa 1885*. (Track width 2½″.) Note the slotted side rods which are a quaint toy-makers' solution to the problem arising from single-acting oscillating cylinders driving crank pins 180° apart.
Photo Udel Studios   E. Hoffman Collection

4 A Weedon 'Dart' 0–4–0 and tender in live steam, together with a Pullman car of the same manufacture. Gauge 2, *circa 1890*.
Photo Udel Studios   E. Hoffman Collection

5

6

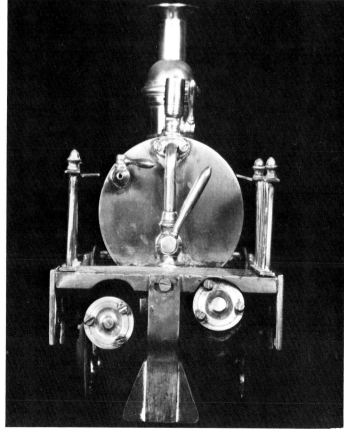

7

5 Two of the best, in live steam, by Newton & Co. A 3¾″ gauge, fixed radius, 2–2–2 locomotive (standing on original track with separate cast brass rails and chairs) and a 2¾″ gauge 2–2–0. Both with beautifully finished pierced brass sheet frames, twin inside oscillating cylinders, ebony buffer beams and turned footplate railings. *Circa 1875* and very much the work of scientific instrument makers.   J. Minns Collection

6 A selection of goods wagons, vans and passenger coaches marketed by Stevens's Model Dockyard for their pre-1900 live steam locomotives.

7 Backhead of Newton 2–2–0 (as illustrated above), with twin oscillating cylinders.   J. Minns Collection

1   In the foreground a Stevens's Model Dockyard, $2\frac{3}{8}''$ gauge 2–2–0, *circa 1880*. Partly illustrated in the background is a fine 4″ gauge 4–4–0 and tender, 'Greater Britain,' *circa 1890*. The contemporary prices of these steam locomotives was five shillings and £7 respectively, and the little 2–2–0, despite its antiquity, continued in production until 1912.   P. Minns Collection

2   In this model virtually standard locomotive parts have been carefully added to by the Stereoscopic Co. of London to make a very interestingly accurate, live steam model land locomotive or traction engine, with the front steersman so typical of the first traction engines of the 1840's and 1850's. Fabricated frames are supported on cast bearing blocks, and the capstan steered front wheels have unique stub axles. (Track width 3″.)
Photo Udel Studios   E. Hoffman Collection

3   Typical of the less mass-produced brass live steam locomotives, this $3\frac{1}{2}''$ gauge, 2–2–2 twin inside oscillating cylinder locomotive and train set by W. Wilson is beautifully made. 'Firebrand' has fabricated brass frames, filler dome and safety valves, and the hand-painted 1st and 2nd class coaches, like the locomotive, have axles set for the circular, cast-brass, numbered track so often supplied with mid-nineteenth century sets.
         J. Minns Collection

4 Here is a 3¾″ gauge 2–2–2 *piddler*, 'Wellington', which really was made *in toto* by Clyde Model Dockyard and Engine Depot in the 1870's. Clyde were also the main marketers of Radiguet equipment, which they claimed to be 'our latest designs of locomotives, etc'. Cruder even than the cheapest Radiguets, the locomotive illustrated, sold with solid cast frames, railing and fittings is one of the best examples of English primitive style locomotives.

4

5 This fine 3¾″ gauge, 2–2–2 locomotive in live steam, was one of the largest produced by the famous Parisian instrument makers, Radiguet et Massiot, in the 1880's. Radiguet produced many parts for the English companies, which claimed to have manufactured them themselves, and those companies even marketed complete Parisian locomotives as their own. This one has many elaborate fittings – open cast frames, rivetted boiler endplates and true Stephenson's link motion. (The stove pipe chimney, while following the correct pattern is not original.)
J. Minns Collection

6 Grand names full of 'pomp' were a prerequisite for any self-respecting model locomotive of the Victorian era, illustrating this is part of a fine 3⅞″ gauge, live steam 2–2–2 'Duke of Edinburgh' – all well primed for a 'right royal explosion' – by the British Modelling and Electrical Company, *circa 1885*. These locomotives included fixed outside cylinders, Stephenson's link gear, level test cocks and japanned boiler.
J. Minns Collection

6

5

2 A fine, middle-sized, live steam, Great Western $2\frac{5}{8}''$ gauge model, 4–2–2 Well Tank locomotive no. 554, 'Boadicea', by Stevens's Model Dockyard, *circa 1886*. This was found with two mahogany trucks, and is a clear example of an early attempt to get away from the primitive Victorian prototypes and produce a reasonably accurate model. All the fittings and lamps are British made, and the valves are slip-eccentric controlled. The backhead of this locomotive (fig. 1) appears to have been hewn out of the solid, but then charm was not an attribute of the later Dockyard models, which incorporated many rough castings.

J. Minns Collection

3 Small American cast iron 2–2–0 floor train, possibly by Kenton, *circa 1900*. (Track width 1⅛″.)

4 Wallwork's metal foundry in Manchester, produced as one of their ancillary lines, a series of cast iron floor trains, none of which appeared to have mechanisms. However, proof exists that some of the locomotives were finished with coupling rods. Legend has it that these trains were modelled very loosely on those which ran past the works, but there is no evidence that the types produced bore anything but a fleeting resemblance to any particular railway of that period. *Circa 1892.* As cast iron trains of English manufacture they were unique. Illustrated is a passenger set. (Track width 2⅜″.)

5 A typical cast iron saloon car ascribed to Kenton, *circa 1900*. This car formed part of a set comprising a 4–4–0 locomotive and tender, plus another car. (Track width 2½″.)

1

1 American pull train in cast iron by J. & E. Stevens Co., *circa 1890*. (Track width 2⅛".) The impression given is of some prehistoric creature being hauled from the depths, and in this it is illustrative of the extremely primitive quality of early American toy trains. It also emphasises the American love of cast iron toys, which was virtually unique to North America.

3 Hearts in the driving wheels, flowers on the boiler, embossed stars and the name, 'Combat', formed the decoration to this 0–2–2 clockwork Fallows tin train (the actual working wheel arrangement is in fact in the form of a tricycle). *Circa 1890*. An engraving of a similar toy listed by Althof Bergmann and Company, *circa 1874* appears below. (Track width 3⅜".)

2

2 A goods train by Wallwork for floor running, *circa 1892*. (Track width 2⅜".)

3

4 Primitive, hand-painted Märklin, *circa 1895*, in the form of a gauge 0, clockwork 0–2–2 and tender, with coaches and postal coach of the period. These early Märklin locomotives were seldom fitted with outside motion, and the earliest 0 gauge examples can be recognised by the simulated spokes cast in relief onto the solid driving wheels, these being picked out with thin brush strokes. A further typical feature of these early clockwork locomotives was a hand-painted pressure-gauge in the cab.   M. Darphin Collection

5 An 0 gauge 0–4–0, clockwork locomotive and tender depicted with one of its original coaches, by FV, *circa 1895*. M. Darphin Collection

1

1 A magnificent 2–2–0 and tender in clockwork for gauge 2, together with its original coaches. This train is believed to be the work of Schoenner, though at the present time this assignation cannot be considered conclusive. *Circa 1890.*   M. Darphin Collection

2 A gauge 1 version of the train illustrated on page 17, (fig. 4), once again in clockwork. The coaches and wagons are typical of gauge 1 stock of that time. Märklin, *circa 1895.*   S. Darphin Collection

2

3 A unique, steam powered 0–4–0 and tender by Märklin
for gauge 2, *circa 1897*. The boiler was fired by a blow-lamp
arrangement in the cab, although this system did not last
beyond the turn of the century. It would be fair to assume
that safety requirements were not of much moment when
this little monster was produced.
Photo Udel Studios   E. Hoffman Collection

4 The original box top of this little 0 gauge, clockwork train
set by Issmayer (JAJ), *circa 1895*, has been used as the
cover picture, and it is typical of the amazing difference
between box top illustration and actual content. It is
interesting to note that the winged wheel motif, in the top
left-hand corner of the illustration, was also used as a
trade mark – in a slightly amended form – by the firms of
Ernst Plank and Gebr. Bing.

5 One of the first interpretations of hydraulic buffers, and a
unique triangular junction by Bing, *circa 1895*. The Bing
gauge 0, live steam locomotive with external flywheel is
coupled to a Märklin water wagon. *Circa 1900*.
                                                    R. McCrindell Collection

1 The products of Bing and Märklin, both catalogued in 1895, meet in this picture. The dockside train is a gauge 2, live steam 2–2–0 together with its original vans, and displays the very earliest embossed trade mark used by Bing. HMS 'Terrible', a steam powered ship by Märklin, lies in dry dock.   R. McCrindell Collection

2 A mystery floor train, displaying the trade mark 'R & GN' (Richards and Gebrüder Nuremburg?). (Track width $1\frac{9}{16}''$.) The set was discovered with its original box, and suggests an early attempt to imitate contemporary Märklin products, *circa 1900*. (Gustav Reder writes that a version of this train, with flanged wheels, for gauge 1 also exists.)   M. Darphin Collection

3 A child's pull train, *circa 1900*, in wood with metal wheels, styled loosely on the GER 'T19' Class. The maker is unknown, but this type of toy was the forerunner of the wooden pull toys that were later marketed by Lines during the embryo days of the Triang Empire. (Track width $4\frac{1}{4}''$.)

4 Two early push toys. Could fig. 4, possibly be described as an American 0–6–0? In any event, it is very gay, without motor and typically French, by HR, *circa 1900*.
The little friction drive 2–2–0 (fig. 5) was driven by a flywheel, brought up to propulsion speed by spinning the knob. Although individual parts of this toy are familiar, it has not been possible to name the manufacturer with any degree of certainty. *Circa 1895*. (Track widths $2\frac{7}{8}''$ and $1\frac{3}{8}''$ respectively.)

THE EDWARDIAN ERA

AND THE DEVELOPMENT OF PROTOTYPE MODELS

1   A spirit fired 3¼″ gauge 'Johnson' 4–4–0 and tender by Bassett-Lowke, *circa 1903*. This model was unique in that virtually all the body construction was comprised of castings. It is doubtful whether any other British-made commercial model was produced with a fully cast tender body. It was available as a set of parts or as a finished model.

This period was later to be known as 'The Golden Age of Model Railways', and the accolade is fully deserved when one considers the quality of its surviving products.

The Anglo-German collaboration of Bassett-Lowke with Bing (under-pinned by the very close personal friendship of the two principals) created some of the finest, quantity-produced, prototype models. So good, in fact, was this link that goods ready for shipment from Bingwerke to Bassett-Lowke in 1914 completed their journey after the end of hostilities in 1918 on the pre-war delivery terms. It is for this reason that certain Bing-made items were available in England long after their actual production ceased.

Märklin graduated during the early 1900's from the production of fantasy and freelance locomotives and rolling stock to the manufacture of models styled more closely on existing prototypes. Their interpretations at that time were still only loosely

linked with reality, and in the case of English prototypes, they certainly lacked the guidance Henry Greenly was able – from 1907 onwards – to bring to Bing's work in that field. Nonetheless, Märklin items of this era have a very distinct aura to them, and there is little doubt that in collecting terms they rank very highly with their contemporaries. My own theory, however, is that in the fullness of time, Bing's work for Bassett-Lowke, particularly during the period 1907–1914, will be seen to be one of the most important advances in the art of commercial modelling of contemporary prototypes.

Georges Carette of Nuremberg extended his traditional range and, from 1905, produced many excellent lithographed coaches and wagons for the English market, in addition to a limited range of locomotives, and once again this work stemmed from very close personal ties with W. J. Bassett-Lowke. Carette's locomotives of this period were to be

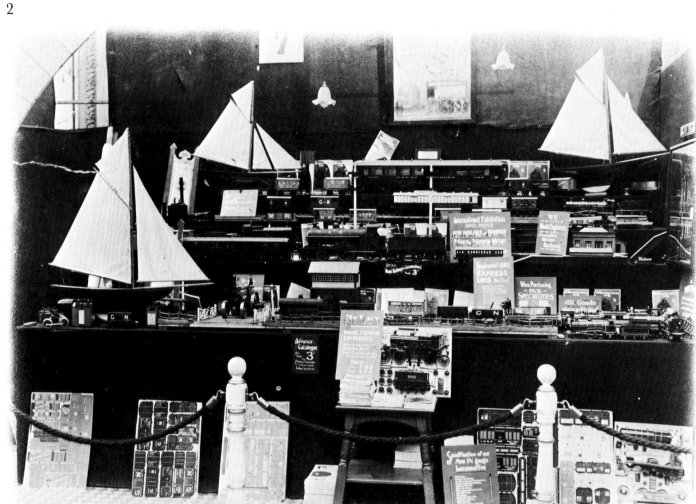

2 Bassett-Lowke's stand at the Model Engineer Exhibition, October, 1909.

remembered more for their invention and superb appearance than for their operating efficiency. Although by 1917 Carette & Cie were no longer in business, their contribution to the art of photolithography as applied to tinplate trains was not to be surpassed before the plastic age, some 45 years later, sounded the effective death knell of that marvellous medium.

It is apparent at this time that the British model railway market were predominant in both interest and spending power, certainly so far as Europe was concerned and particularly during the pre-1914 period. The causes were complex and are beyond the scope of this work. The effect, however, was patent, in that a relatively high percentage of German model train production was fashioned almost exclusively for the British market. It is for this reason that a large proportion of the illustrations in this section relates to British prototypes. Almost all these models, despite several explicit claims to the contrary, originated in German factories.

The years before the first world war were the last in which relative free trade allowed European manufacturers to penetrate the American market with extremely cheap toy trains. After 1918 Bing was one of the few German manufacturers to regain a significant foothold in this market, and this was achieved apparently at the expense of producing items which resembled products of existing US manufacturers, particularly Ives. All this time Ives and Lionel were at work creating their own *folklore*, aspects of which will be touched upon when we deal with a later period.

The pre-1914 era did not see the emergence of any British-based manufacturing concerns of importance, and although Hornby's clockwork trains, thought to have been manufactured at that time by Carette and marketed under the name 'Raylo', appeared briefly in 1915, their full impact was not to be felt until the turn of the decade. The period witnessed the final decline of the pioneering British firms who specialised in the manufacture of brass steam locomotives. Despite the fierce challenges which they threw down in public, and especially in the prefaces to their catalogues, both Clyde Model Dockyard, (who continued trading as a retail establishment until about 1970) and, in 1926, Stevens's Model Dockyard ceased manufacturing, being unable to withstand the strong competition from the Continent.

Other names known to collectors also disappeared, such as Carette, and Schoenner, so that the two giants, Märklin and Bing, were to enter the 1920's virtually unchallenged in Europe, although Bing was to be swept away in the economic and political overtures to the 1930's.

1 Typical bazaar 'penny toy' floor train (without mechanism) thought to be by Hess, *circa 1904* (track width $\frac{15}{16}''$), alongside a toy ship by Georg Levy. Bing, Carette and Issmayer listed very similar trains, and it would not be surprising if all these firms acted as sub-contractors to one another at various times.

2 Clockwork gauge 0, 4–2–0 and coach by C. Rossignol, *circa 1910*. This train is typical of the very primitive designs perpetuated well into the 1920's by this firm, particularly with its range of large clockwork floor trains. There is little evidence to suggest that the firm ever concerned itself with scale railways in however loose a form.

MODEL RAILWAY TONNAGE

Gauge No. 00 ($\frac{5}{8}''$)		
1 scale ton =	088 ozs. of model.	1 lb. of model = 180 tons.
Gauge No. 0 ($1\frac{1}{4}''$)		
1 scale ton =	·55 ,, ,,	,, ,, ,, = 29 ,,
Gauge No. 1 ($1\frac{3}{4}''$)		
1 scale ton =	1·23 ,, ,,	,, ,, ,, = 13 ,,
Gauge No. 2 (2″)		
1 scale ton =	2·28 ,, ,.	,, ,, ,, = 7 ,,
Gauge No. 3 ($2\frac{1}{2}''$)		
1 scale ton =	2·95 ,, ,,	,, ,, ,, = 5·41 ,,
$\frac{11}{16}''$ scale. Gauge $3\frac{1}{4}''$		
1 scale ton =	·416 lb. ,,	,, ,, ,, = 2·4 ,,
1″ scale. Gauge $4\frac{13}{16}''$		
1 scale ton =	1·29 ,, ,,	,, ,, ,, = ·775 tons.
$1\frac{1}{2}''$ scale. Gauge $7\frac{1}{4}''$		
1 scale ton =	4·37 ,, ,,	1 cwt. ,, ,, = 25·6 ,,
2″ scale. Gauge $9\frac{1}{2}''$		
1 scale ton =	10 4 ,, ,,	,, ,, ,, = 10·3 ,,

15″ Gauge passenger locomotive is 1/60 to 1/50 weight of prototype.

PARTICULARS OF RAILS.

3

NO O	35mm $1\frac{3}{8}''$
NO 1	48mm $1\frac{7}{8}''$
NO 2	54mm $2\frac{1}{8}''$
NO 3	67mm $2\frac{5}{8}''$
NO 4	75mm $2\frac{15}{16}''$

This illustration shews exact Gauge in Section of our Standard Rails.

Particulars of our Standard Size Curved Rails, as follows:

No. 0—1¼in. Gauge. 10in. long. 6 pieces to circle, 1ft. 8in. outside dia.
No. 1—1¾in. ,,   14in. ,,   8   ,,   3ft. 0in. ,,
No. 2—2in.   ,,   14¼in. ,, 12   ,,   4ft. 6in. ,,
No. 3—2½in. ,,   14½in. ,, 12   ,,   4ft. 8in. ,,
No. 4—3in.   ,,   14½in. ,, 16   ,,   6ft. 2in. ,,

Straight Rails same length as curved.

When ordering Rails for Locos. or Coaches of other makers, please measure as shown and we will make the necessary allowance.

MEASURE HERE

4 A Märklin canopied station sets the scene which includes two gauge 1, live steam, Carette 'Singles', *circa 1902*. The example at right, was restored by Littledale. Also illustrated is an extremely rare clerestory postal car by Bing, *circa 1898*. The station accessories include an early booking hall and ticket machine by Märklin, and a red ticket rack by Bing, including original tickets. The tinplate bus is by Lehmann.

5 An example of very robust Märklin, in the form of an LSWR 0–4–0 and tender, in live steam, for gauge 0 (see also fig. 1, page 26), *circa 1903*.   Torry Collection

1 This model is believed to be the gauge 0 derivative of Märklin's 'Decapods' (prototype GER 0–10–0 Tank locomotive). This compact little steam engine, *circa 1905*, is typical of a whole series of very robust 0–4–0's incorporating two valves per cylinder, produced by Märklin at this time. The model illustrated in Gamage's advertisement is noticeably different from a gauge 2 version (see engraving) as advertised by Bassett-Lowke in their 1904 catalogue. To further confuse the issue, one of the few gauge 1 examples of this locomotive to come to light in recent years was nominally a 6–4–0, i.e. it displayed a six-wheeled leading bogie. As far as one can ascertain, a true 0–10–0 version of this locomotive was not commercially produced.   Torry Collection

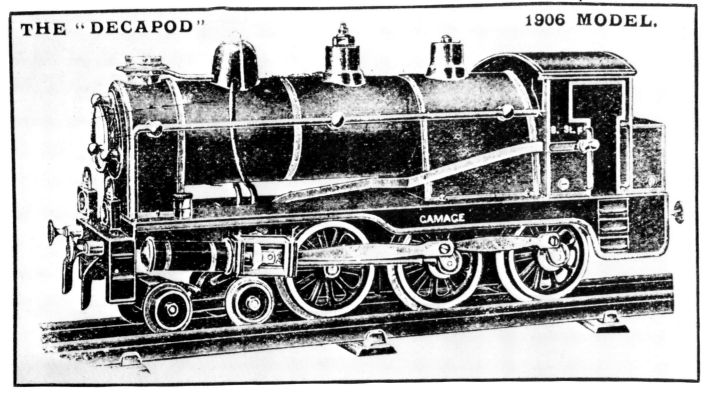

1

THE "DECAPOD"   1906 MODEL.

GAMAGE

3 A live steam train by Plank for gauge 1, *circa 1908*, descends the ramp after crossing a swing bridge (Bing). A gauge 1, single driver by Carette, *circa 1902*, cools off in a siding.

2

2 A Bing steam locomotive for gauge 2, *circa 1904*. This model vaguely suggests an early Ivatt rebuild of the 'Stirling Single' and it heads a rake of three heavy-gauge metal GNR coaches of the period by Bing. Both locomotive and coaches were hand-enamelled. The bogies used with this particular tender normally comprised a pressing utilising half of the standard British-type coach bogie. The tender as illustrated, however, appears to be fitted with Bing Continental coach bogies which are probably not original. (*For Bassett-Lowke*)

3

1 Gauge 3 ($2\frac{15}{16}''$ – equivalent to Bing's gauge 4) was the
largest of Märklin's gauges for which locomotives and
rolling stock were produced in any quantity. This
magnificent example of a Great Northern 4–4–0 and
tender, in live steam, *circa 1903*, together with Great
Northern coaches of the period, is given scale by the little
Bing set (see fig. 1. page 30) in what might be described as
'medieval' N gauge.   Torry Collection

2

2 Diminutive Plank live steam locomotive in gauge 1, *circa 1904,* with a typical nineteenth century 2nd Class carriage, by Märklin, *circa 1895.*

4 Front end of gauge 2 Bing live steam 'Pilot', displaying the embossed trade mark on the smokebox door, a feature of early Bing and Märklin locomotives. *Circa 1902.* (*For Bassett-Lowke*)

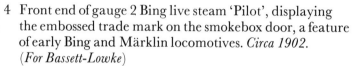

4

5

3

3 An extremely rare Lancashire and Yorkshire 4–4–0 in gauge 2, live steam, by Bing *circa 1902.* The drive is by way of twin oscillating, single acting cylinders mounted between the frames. The outside coupling rods were omitted in the interests of free running. (*For Bassett-Lowke*)

5 Cab end of Bing live steam, North London Railway Tank for gauge 2, *circa 1904.* (*For Bassett-Lowke*)

1 A Midland version of Bing's famous 'Black Prince' series
for gauge 3 in live steam, *circa 1908*. This example is one of
the last of the series which commenced in 1901, prior to
the introduction of the scale model 'Black Prince' in 1909.
(No Midland variant of the latter model was made.)
Contrast this with the marvellous non-mechanised
LNWR 'George V' tin-lithographed set by Bing, *circa
1912*. (See also fig. 1, page 28.) It is believed that these sets
were produced primarily for advertising purposes. (Track
width ⅜″.) *(For Bassett-Lowke)*   Torry Collection

2 'Black Prince' by Plank for gauge 2, in live steam, *circa
1903*. These engines were obviously sold to compete with
the Bing 'Black Prince' series, which reinforces the theory
that the English model train market was an extremely
lucrative one for Continental manufacturers in this period,
particularly in the absence of any serious home-based
competition. Future historians may wish to pursue the
suggestion that many of the parts used in this locomotive
shared a common manufacturer with Bing.
Photo Udel Studios   E. Hoffman Collection

5 Engraving of an LSWR 4–4–0 in live steam, for 3″ gauge
by Schoenner, *circa 1904*. (To date no example of this
model has been seen, despite extensive enquiries.)

6 Engravings of a saloon coach and luggage van believed
to be by Schoenner, *circa 1900*.

3

4

3 If one had to choose a model that typified the Edwardian style, I would have little hesitation in choosing this superb 3″ gauge SECR 4–4–0 and tender, (loosely based on the inside cylinder 'Wainwright D' prototype) in live steam, by Schoenner, *circa 1903*. I doubt if more than a handful of this maker's larger engines were ever produced. The particular example illustrated is completely original and of enormous importance. Other items by this manufacturer were marketed by Bassett-Lowke, but it is doubtful whether this was on an exclusive basis.

Photo Lewis Studios   M. Roberts Collection

4 Yet another live steam 'Black Prince', this time for gauge 3 by Schoenner, *circa 1905*. W. E. Finlason writes: 'Shortly after the turn of the century Schoenner produced several 4–4–0 type locomotives, but in reality they tended to have one driving axle only because there were no side rods. Most of these locomotives include such peculiarities as a reversing block recessed into the underside of the boiler, controlled by a lever mounted alongside the cab, and elaborate lubricators fitted to the front ends of the cylinders.' For further examples see SECR 4–4–0 (fig. 3) and the PLM 'Coupe Vent' (fig. 7).   Torry Collection

7 'Coupe Vent' in live steam by Schoenner for 3″ gauge, *circa 1903*. Illustrations of this locomotive have often appeared in the form of the original catalogue engraving and this picture of an actual example is a remarkable illustration of an early attempt at commercial scale modelling by this fascinating and yet somewhat obscure manufacturer.

Photo Bommer   Petiet Collection

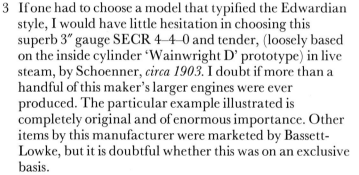

5

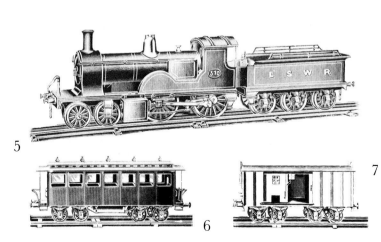

6

7

A Unique Method of Advertising.

THE OIL CAN.

Another Bassett-Lowke Triumph.

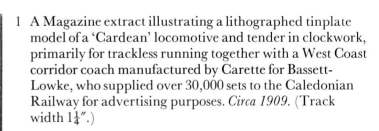

Model Railways

A Fascinating Hobby for Young and Old.

HAVING made the production of working models our special study, and equipped our works with the latest machinery, we are able to offer the very best goods at a moderate cost, and can fit up a complete Model Railway for a Drawing-room Table, or a Miniature Railway to carry passengers round a Park. These form

Ideal Xmas Presents

Complete Catalogue, No. 63, over 300 pages, post free 7d. Send postcard for booklet :: :: ::

'Run Your Own Train Service.'

BASSETT-LOWKE, Ltd., NORTHAMPTON
London Branch : 112, HIGH HOLBORN, W.C.

1 A Magazine extract illustrating a lithographed tinplate model of a 'Cardean' locomotive and tender in clockwork, primarily for trackless running together with a West Coast corridor coach manufactured by Carette for Bassett-Lowke, who supplied over 30,000 sets to the Caledonian Railway for advertising purposes. *Circa 1909.* (Track width 1¼″.)

3 An illustration taken from 'The Oil Can' Bassett-Lowke's trade insert in 'Models, Railways and Locomotives' edited by Henry Greenly, shows a 2½″ gauge North Eastern 4–4–0 in live steam, incorporating a semi-flash boiler by Carson for Bassett-Lowke. The nine locomotives illustrated in the course of assembly comprise virtually the whole production line of this short-lived design. *Circa 1913.*

4

2 The 'Lady of the Lake' in gauge 1 by Carette, *circa 1903*, was the first quantity produced live steam model made to anything resembling scale proportions. Despite the relatively large number produced, it has become an extremely rare item for collectors. (As noted in the bibliography, 'Bassett-Lowke's 50 Years of Modelling' states erroneously that this locomotive preceded the Bing 'Black Prince' in 1901.)
(For Bassett-Lowke)   Torry Collection

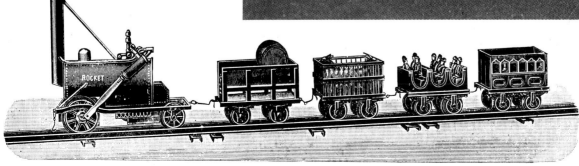

4 Of all the great German manufacturers, only Märklin were to produce a model of Stephenson's 'Rocket', *circa 1903*, and it would appear to be the only commercially produced, live steam model, ever attempted. This example with its original train for gauge 1, is one of the few complete trains to come to light in recent years.
A. Bommer Collection

1 One of the lasting fascinations of collecting old trains is that when all appears to have been revealed, fresh discoveries come to light. Such a discovery is this Great Northern 'Single' in live steam ascribed to Bing, for gauge 1, *circa 1902*. The smokebox assembly, including the cylinder covers, is very similar to that eventually used by Bing in its model of the North London Tank. On the other hand, the valance over the pony truck is very much in the style of Carette. This item does not appear to have been catalogued.

1 *Photo Udel Studios*   E. Hoffman Collection

2 A live steam, gauge 1, 4–4–0 and tender based on the Great Eastern 'Claud Hamilton' by Carette, *circa 1905*. As with so many Carette locomotives of this time, considerable use has been made of heavy metal castings. This particular example has been completely restored.

Count Giansanti Collection

3 Two examples of Carette's most superb 'Vauclains' for gauge 1. At left, a clockwork version with a unique simulation of the valve gear driven off the leading axle. At right, the high-stepping steam version, incorporating one of Carette's many strange valve gear designs (which are regrettably hidden from sight), of marvellous complexity, but doubtful efficiency. Both locomotives, *circa 1905*.   Torry Collection

4 A 2½″ gauge GNR 'Stirling Single' by Carette in live steam, *circa 1902*, draws into the station with a Bing GNR coach. (In reality this was the correct load for this locomotive, since owing to the extensive use of heavy metal castings, the power-to-weight ratio was somewhat inadequate.) Along with the Carette limousine awaiting its passenger, the scene conveys the very essence of the period of Edwardian tinplate trains. The station is by Märklin (when did the GNR ever run through Richmond?).
(For Bassett-Lowke)   Torry Collection

4

1 This 4–4–0 and tender by Märklin for gauge 1 was one of
the earliest series of electrically powered steam outline
locomotives. High voltage electric motors were first fitted
to these Märklin models in 1904, and the 4–4–0 illustrated
is a development of these first series electric engines. It was
produced in this form during the 1906/9 period.
                                                    O. Baur Collection

2 A Contractor's locomotive by Bing for gauge 4, in live
steam, *circa 1904*. This remarkable locomotive is driven
by a single oscillating cylinder located in the smokebox,
transferring its drive to the leading axle through a series
of reduction gears. Although examples of single cab
mounted oscillating cylinders were to be found later,
Bing did not persevere with the earlier system.
(For Bassett-Lowke)

3 An extremely rare gauge 1 clockwork model of De Glehn's 'La France' by Märklin, *circa 1906*. Märklin finished the model in the original prototype livery as delivered to the Great Western Railway, i.e. – black with brick red lining of enclosed panels, longitudinal lining in white and cylinder lining in grey.
Photo B. Hinchley   B. Hinchley Collection

4 'Night Express' to Cannes comprising a Märklin PLM gauge 0, clockwork 'Coupe Vent' and appropriate PLM cars, *circa 1907*.   Count Giansanti Collection

5 Another version of the 'Coupe Vent', this time in steam for gauge 1. Also illustrated is an unusual 'Postes et Télégraphes' car, *circa 1909*, all items by Märklin.
                    Count Giansanti Collection

1 A rare model of a 'Westinghouse' electric locomotive for the Metropolitan Railway Company, in gauge 1 by Carette, *circa 1908*. The 4–6 volt motor was an integral part of one of the bogies and drove the locomotive by friction onto the four wheels of one truck. The design of this model locomotive was very much Henry Greenly's, although he had left the Metropolitan Railways' employ as a draughtsman shortly before this prototype was introduced in 1904.
(For Bassett-Lowke) O. Baur Collection

2

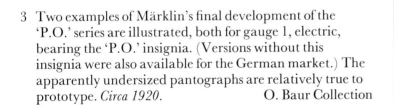

2 Bing's gauge 0 version of the first Central London Railway, electric train, *circa* 1904. Unlike Märklin, Bing's early electric outline locomotives were lithographed.

3 Two examples of Märklin's final development of the 'P.O.' series are illustrated, both for gauge 1, electric, bearing the 'P.O.' insignia. (Versions without this insignia were also available for the German market.) The apparently undersized pantographs are relatively true to prototype. *Circa 1920*. O. Baur Collection

4 At left, an early gauge 0 'Steeplecab' in electric, at right, a clockwork version of a Central London Railway 'Steeplecab' in gauge 1, both *circa 1904*, by Märklin.
O. Baur Collection

5 This model represents the first attempt by Märklin to model an electric prototype locomotive, and it derived its basic shape from the first locomotives used by the Central London Railway, known as the 'Twopenny Tube'.

Ironically, when first introduced this locomotive was available in clockwork only, although Märklin had already marketed electrically powered tramway systems. Gauge 1, *circa 1901*. A. Bommer Collection

6 The electric locomotives depicted became known by the generic term of 'P.O.', and indeed this type of locomotive was originally introduced for working between 'Paris–Austerlitz' and 'Paris–Orsay'. They were also known as 'Steeplecabs'. The two gauge 1 examples illustrated are both by Märklin. The model on the left, introduced to depict the Central London Railway Bo Bo, is in this instance finished in the livery of the Paris/Orleans, *circa 1904*. The locomotive on the right is a later example, again in 'P.O.' designation, *circa 1912*. O. Baur Collection

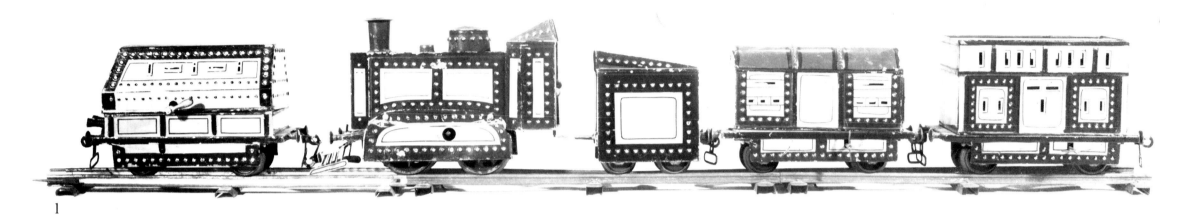

1 A very unwarlike armoured train in clockwork, for
gauge 1, by Märklin, *circa 1904*, inspired by those in
service for the British army during the Boer War.
Photo Lewis Studios   M. Roberts Collection

2 A gauge 1 version of a District Line twin-car set by
Märklin, in clockwork, circa 1902. (Note early type bogie
frames), a gauge 0 version appears in fig. 3.
Photo Lewis Studios   M. Roberts Collection

3

3 Inter-urban and underground model trains might easily form a subject in themselves. Many of these items are extremely rare as they did not appear to enjoy the popularity of their steam outlined counterparts. This gauge 0 District Railway set by Märklin is an early example of the *genre* in clockwork, *circa 1906*.
Count Giansanti Collection

4

4 Uncatalogued non-motorised, New York streetcar set by Märklin for gauge 0, *circa 1912*. (There did not appear to be a contemporary power bogie by Märklin for this model.) Count Giansanti Collection

5

5 Paris Metro set in gauge 1 electric by Märklin, *circa 1908*.
Count Giansanti Collection

1 Front end of Günthermann clockwork floor tram, *circa 1910*. (Track width 1¾″.)

2 A British tramcar for gauge 1 by Bing in electric, displaying impaled, but seemingly content, passengers, mostly by Märklin, *circa 1906*.

R. McCrindell Collection

3 Carette's extremely rare three-car electric underground railway set, for gauge 1, introduced in 1911.

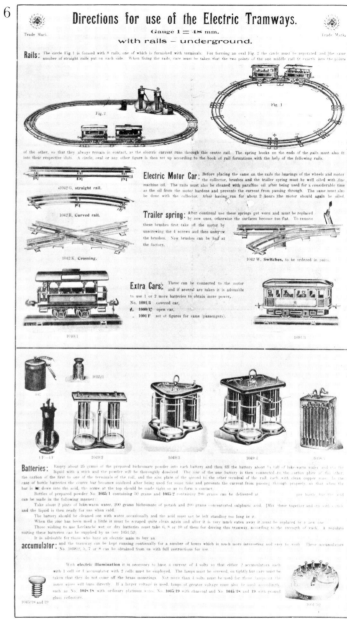

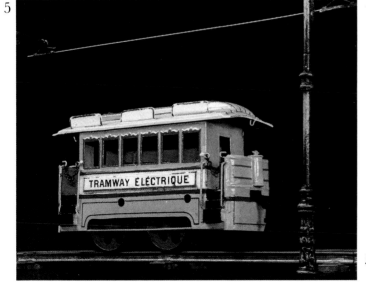

4 Twin car tram unit by Märklin for gauge 1, clockwork, *circa 1904*, with imitation overhead wiring system.

A. Bommer Collection

6 Instruction sheet for early electric tramway set by Carette, *circa 1904*.

5 A primitive Märklin 'Streetcar' in clockwork, for gauge 1, *circa 1902*. A. Bommer Collection

1

1 Experimental design for the Prussian State Railway was
this ultimate 'Windcutter', designed by Wittfeld and
built by Henschel, which Märklin were to catalogue as the
'Kassel Hannover Express' locomotive, *circa 1904*, for
gauge 1. Unquestionably one of the most extraordinary
live steam locomotives ever produced by Märklin, even
though they chose to overlook a tender for this engine.
It is not surprising that amongst Märklin collectors
this item ranks as one of the most highly sought after. (The
design of the prototype locomotive has also been ascribed
to one named Kuhn, although the name Wittfeld appears
in an official Henschel works listing.)
Photo Lewis Studios   M. Roberts Collection

2

4

4 0–4–0 Tank engine in clockwork, by Märklin for gauge 1,
circa 1902.   A. Bommer Collection

3

2 Two gauge 1 Verandah cars based on those used in early
days on the Swiss Gotthardbahn. At left, the Märklin
version, *circa 1905* coupled to the more delicate Bing car,
circa 1902.   M. Darphin Collection

3 Gauge 0 carriages by Märklin, *circa 1903,* to complement
the little Central London Railway 'Steeplecab'
locomotive. (Fig. 4, page 39.)   A. Bommer Collection

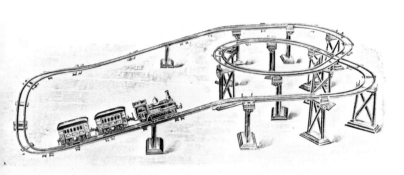

2 Gauge 2 Märklin 'Steeplecab' for electric rack-railway operation with 'Observation' car. *Circa 1908.*

A. Bommer Collection

1 In order to trace the development of Märklin's Rack-Railway locomotives to their conclusion, the last 20 volt A.C. electric version in gauge 1, *circa 1929*, is illustrated above, (Märklin introduced its 20 volt A.C. system in 1926) reversed on to a Märklin coach, *circa 1904*. At right, one of the earliest gauge 0 electric rack locomotives 'on the rack', *circa 1908*.   A. Bommer Collection

3

3 Two gauge 1 versions of 'Kaiser Train' cars coupled to a
'Red Cross' vehicle. Märklin, *circa 1901*.
A. Bommer Collection

4

4 Turn-of-the-century 'Kaiser Train' comprising cars
bearing the Kaiser's crown emblem, for gauge 0, awaits
motive power. The little green four-wheel carriage is
another extremely rare example of hand-painted
Märklin work of this period.

1 If anything, an even more attractive version of the 'Kaiser Train' cars with unusual gothic windows, in gauge 1, this time by Bing, *circa 1902*. The postal car which appeared with this train is depicted in fig. 4, page 25.
A. Bommer Collection

2 Early hand-painted Märklin work in gauge 1 for the British market in the form of two LNWR clerestory coaches, *circa 1903*. This coach design was primarily of Continental pattern, and these particular coaches were also turned out in Midland, GNR and LSWR liveries.
R. McCrindell Collection

3

4

3 Three rare Märklin gauge 1 four-wheel carriages. Left to right, green German carriage made for one year only, *circa 1908,* two-deck Paris suburban carriage, *circa 1908,* and German carriage, *circa 1905.*　　O. Baur Collection

4 A pair of 'Congressional' cars for the American market in gauge 1, by Märklin, *circa 1908.*　　O. Baur Collection

1

1 An example of a basic Märklin 4–4–0 chassis and tender, *circa 1906,* with an American style superstructure in clockwork for gauge 1. Standard Continental cars together with a 'Red Cross' vehicle make up the train, *circa 1903.* (Louis Hertz writes: 'Märklin's 3-window U.S. type cab derives from the Ives cab of 1901. For some considerable time Märklin were under the false impression that all U.S. locomotives had 3-window cabs.')
Photo Udel Studios   E. Hoffman Collection

2

2 A gauge 2 Beggs 2–2–2 live steam, locomotive and tender, designed for continuous curve running, together with two tinplate and pasteboard cars by that firm, *circa 1901.*
Photo Udel Studios   E. Hoffman Collection

3

3 A live steam 4–4–0 and tender in gauge 2 by McNair, *circa 1910.* This little firm would appear to have been the successor to Beggs, and like so many small American firms specialising in live steam engines, it was to enjoy a relatively brief hour upon the scene.
Photo Udel Studios   E. Hoffman Collection

4 A cow catcher and a bell were all that appeared to be required to restyle a European locomotive for the American market. This little gauge 0 clockwork 0–4–0 and tender by Märklin, *circa 1903*, is a charming example of such a conversion, although the two 'Congressional' cars are somewhat more convincing.

Count Giansanti Collection

5 Another glimpse of Dr. Bommer's collection this time featuring what must have been the largest steam locomotive ($4\frac{5}{8}''$ gauge) ever manufactured by Märklin, together with its original cars, *circa 1905*. It is not known whether more than one of these American-styled trains were ever produced, and no catalogue record is available for this amazing machine. It is thought that this particular train might have been produced to special order as part of a garden railway. (An LNWR liveried 4–4–0 and tender with three coaches, in a similar gauge, is known to exist.)

6 Garlick, once associated with Beggs, was a pioneer American toy train manufacturer who produced a small batch of these remarkable electric locomotives at the turn of the century.
Photo by courtesy of Louis Hertz and Walter A. Lucas

1 The Swiss firm of Löwenstein appeared to flourish in the
vacuum created during the first world war when the
larger German manufacturers were otherwise engaged.
The example illustrated is a gauge 1, twin-motored
electric BLS locomotive, *circa 1917*. Although no prototype
with this arrangement existed, it was based on the
BLS 0–6–6–0 type, first introduced in 1911. Snow plough
by Märklin, *circa 1902*.   O. Baur Collection

2 Another example of the work of Löwenstein. Illustrated
here is a gauge 1 electric locomotive for the American
market, *circa 1920*.   A. Bommer Collection

3 One of Lionel's early classics for standard gauge was this
1912 'special'.

4

5

4 A superb gauge 1 Pennsylvania 'Class 28' Pacific by Märklin, *circa 1912*. Gustav Reder's comment concerning the placement of the simulated firebox and ashpan directly beneath the cab on this model, is well illustrated, and is a further example of Märklin's artistry, during this period, at the expense of authenticity. The model illustrated is for electric running, and whether this was a factory fitment or subsequent alteration is not clear. The model was marketed in clockwork or electric, with or without inscription on the tender. The Pullman car is also by Märklin, *circa 1908*.
Photo Lewis Studios   M. Roberts Collection

5 Two twin-trucked Bing electric locomotives with cast iron bodies, *circa 1914,* both in gauge 1. Also illustrated is a Märklin gauge 1 'Pabst' car. The locomotives are an example of how German manufacturers adapted themselves to the taste of the American market, with its liking for cast iron. European electric-type locomotives of the same kind would almost invariably be produced in tinplate.   Count Giansanti Collection

1

1 An extremely rare gauge 1 freight train by Märklin in electric for America, *circa 1913.* (Also available in clockwork.)　　　　　　　Count Giansanti Collection

2

2 Americanised Bing 'Pacific' in electric for gauge 1. Also illustrated is a Bing 48.5 cm car bearing the name 'Mississippi', *circa 1912.*　　　Count Giansanti Collection

3 One of Märklin's earliest trains for America. This was available in gauge 1 and gauge 2 at the turn of the century.

3

4

4 A live steam American style 0–4–0 and tender, *circa 1904*, together with early passenger cars by Märklin in gauge 1, *circa 1900*. (Note the similarity of cab design with the large Märklin locomotive, page 51, fig. 5.)
Photo Udel Studios　　　　　　　　　E. Hoffman Collection

6

A RAILWAY
THAT SERVES
AT DINNER

SILVER ENGINE,
COACHES AND
RAILS

A RAJAH'S IDEA

THE State railway of the Maharajah of Gwalior, in the province of Scinde, North-West India, will return home from Britain this week—in a liner.

Then it will resume its function—which is to run round the maharajah's dining table.

It was created by a Northampton firm in 1906, and was the maharajah's own idea. The locomotive is of heavily plated silver, while its seven trucks are dainty silver caskets on wheels, each carrying a glass dish or a decanter.

An electric motor (forty volts) is concealed in the tender, and the train moves slowly round the table on rails of solid silver, which rest on sleepers of polished teak.

Whenever a guest requires anything from the train he lifts out a dish, an act which stops the train. When the dish is replaced the model resumes its journey.

The railway has just had a complete overhaul at the makers, where every part has been cleaned and polished. The word Scindia is in ruby enamel letters.

One of the first banquets at which it will be used will be in celebration of the marriage of the maharajah's daughter.

5 Detail of the lithography on Issmayer's 'Pacific Express Line' car, *circa* 1905.

5

RAILWAY STATION TEA AND

REFRESHMENT WAGGONS.

As will be seen by illustration, these are complete with a full supply of Refreshments, the Waggon is well made, and is mounted on four wheels.

7in. long, 2¼in. wide.

Price, 4/6.

REFRESHMENT TABLE,
GLASSWARE, Etc.

This set, as illustration, consists of Bottles, Decanters, Glasses, Plates, etc.

Price, 2/6.

6 An example of Bassett-Lowke's special work to order as reported in the February 18th edition of the Daily Telegraph, 1934.

1 Live steam 2–2–0 and tender for gauge 0, by Carette, *circa 1905*. Note the use of wheels stamped out of heavy sheet steel, a manufacturing process unique to this maker. Below the same basic design, available for gauge 0 and gauge 1, only this time adapted for the American market, *circa 1911*.

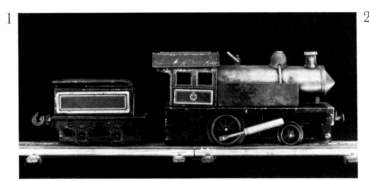

2 A Tank version of fig. 1 in live steam by Carette for gauge 0, *circa 1905*.

3 At left, the elegant LBSCR Tank for gauge 1 electric by Bing, *circa 1911*. At right, Märklin's version of the ex LNWR 'Precursor' Tank (model originally introduced *circa 1909*) in early LMS livery, clockwork for gauge 1. (Bassett-Lowke repaint.) (*LBSCR Tank for Bassett-Lowke*)

4

4 One of the prettiest 0 gauge Tank engines ever produced for the British market was the little clockwork LSWR 'M7' by Bing, *circa 1909*. The scratch built model of Drummonds famous saloon illustrates the different liveries adopted by the LSWR and how Bing's products are such a valuable guide to authentic liveries of the time, bearing in mind the fallibility of memory in this particular area of railway history.
(For Bassett-Lowke)

5 A 2–4–2 Great Western Tank, in clockwork, for gauge 0 by Bing, *circa 1911*. This extremely rare little engine does not appear to have been widely advertised.
(For Bassett-Lowke)

5

1 Two gauge 0 clockwork locomotives by Carette,
illustrating that firm's most distinctive style of lithography.
At left, Midland 4–4–0 and tender, *circa 1911*, to almost
freelance designs; at right, in contrast, GNR 4–4–2
'Atlantic' and tender, *circa 1908*, almost a scale model.
The GNR coaches comprise a short bogie coach by
Carette, *circa 1908*, followed by a similar product by Bing,
circa 1920.

2 This beautiful Great Northern 'Ivatt Single', was one of
the few single drivers to be given scale treatment by a
commercial manufacturer. Clockwork for gauge 1 by
Bing, *circa 1911*. The Great Northern 'Clemenson' coach
of the period was by Carette.
(For Bassett-Lowke)   R. McCrindell Collection

3

3 This gauge 1 clockwork 'Dunalastair' is one of the few models produced by Bing, depicting a Caledonian prototype. Tinplate coaches in Caledonian livery were not manufactured to complement this locomotive. *Circa 1910.*
(For Bassett-Lowke)   Torry Collection

4

4 A Peckett 'Saddle' Tank in clockwork, for gauge 1, with a series of private-owner vans and an LNWR gunpowder van, by Carette, *circa 1909.* The little Tank locomotive (first introduced in 1906) was produced in England from the original tooling during the 1920's.
(For Bassett-Lowke)

2 The history of commercial train manufacturing is full of instances of small firms emerging from obscurity only to disappear whence they came as enthusiasm and individuality were broken on the harsh anvil of commerce. Of the firm of Jubb, it can be said (with due apologies to Jubb *aficionados*) that it 'rose without trace' and disappeared in like manner. The author considers the wooden gauge 0 wagons by Jubb, *circa 1920*, (fig. 1) to be probably amongst the worst rolling stock ever produced. (Ironic in view of the fierce words uttered on the subject of its Continental rivals!) The gauge 1 live steam Great Western 2–4–2 Tank (fig. 3), *circa 1919*, is certainly of a higher order, although the single cylinder between the frames was hardly sufficient to power this relatively heavy locomotive. Perhaps Jubb might best be remembered for their lithographed Great Central coaches for gauge 1 (see page 68, fig. 1) as well as for their employment, at various times, of Henry Greenly of Bassett-Lowke fame, and William Mills, who later founded Milbro.

4 The model in this illustration taken from Jubb's 1919 catalogue, is, in fact, a slightly retouched picture of Bing's classic 'N1' for gauge 1 (see fig. 4, page 87).

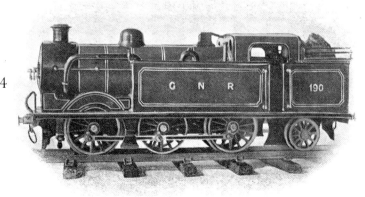

Gauge I., G.N.R., 190., 0-6-2.
STEAM LOCOMOTIVE.

This engine is a model of the well known **G.N.R**, six coupled tank engines used on the Metropoliton Railway, is a very handsome model, which is simple to handle.

5

5 A Bing Midland 'Deeley type' in clockwork, *circa 1909*, for gauge 1, at the head of a rake of Midland clerestory coaches by Carette, *circa 1908*. Down the line is a 'Johnson' Midland 4–4–0 thought to be by Milbro for gauge 1 clockwork, *circa 1920*.
('Deeley type' for Bassett-Lowke)

6

6 One of the most popular gauge 1 locomotives in steam by Bing for Bassett-Lowke was the Great Western 'County of Northampton', *circa 1909*, and the particular example illustrated has been completely restored by C. Littledale. Double-heading with the 'County' is a Bing clockwork Great Western 'Sydney', *circa 1904*. Clerestory full brake by Carette, *circa 1907*.
(For Bassett-Lowke)

1 The 4–4–2 'Tilbury' Tank, *circa 1920*, along with the
'North London' 4–4–0, *circa 1904*, were virtually the only
British prototype Tank models produced in live steam by
Bing, although in 1909 Bassett-Lowke announced the
conversion of the standard Bing-made LNWR 'Precursor'
4–4–2 Tank to steam by fitting a double acting cylinder
between the frames geared to the driving wheels. Two
examples of the 'Tilbury' Tank in gauge 1 are illustrated,
one of them heading a rake of Bing Midland 1st/3rd
coaches, *circa 1921*.
(For Bassett-Lowke)   Torry Collection

2 In the interests of yielding to public sentiment of the time,
manufacturers who had relied to a large extent on the
German model train industry, were careful to disclaim
this connection in their advertising immediately before
and after the first world war. Examples of Bassett-Lowke
advertisements are illustrated and little attempt has been
made to alter the photographic blocks, which clearly
illustrate German-produced items, with copy extolling
the virtues of 'British manufacture'.

3

3 Gauge 1 Bing 'George V' in clockwork, *circa 1911*, pictured with a 'Mulliner' motor van by Carette and LNWR coaches by Märklin, *circa 1907*. The locomotive was also produced in gauge 0 and gauge 2, and after the first world war, the smaller models were sold in a variety of liveries. In retrospect, it seems a little strange that this model was not produced in live steam (perhaps Bing wished to avoid the complications of fixed inside cylinders), but nonetheless, it forms an indispensable part of any collection of the work of Bing's 'Classic Period' from 1907 to 1914.
(For Bassett-Lowke)

4

4 A 'North London' Tank in steam for gauge 1 by Bing, *circa 1904*, with an LNWR 3rd class coach by Bing, *circa 1921*.
(For Bassett-Lowke)   Torry Collection

1 An electric version of a North British 'Atlantic' by Märklin for gauge 1, *circa 1913*.   Torry Collection

2 A clockwork North British 'Atlantic' by Märklin for gauge 1, *circa 1913*. (The leading truck of this locomotive has correct wheels, but incorrect green livery on the spokes.)   Torry Collection

4 An electric version of Märklin's celebrated Great Western 'Great Bear' locomotive in gauge 1, *circa 1909*. Although all versions of this model are extremely rare, it would appear that fewer were produced for electric running.

5 A clockwork 'Great Bear' by Märklin for gauge 1, *circa 1909*.   Torry Collection

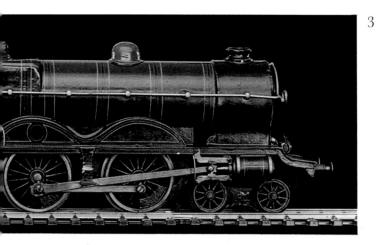

3 A North British 'Atlantic' in live steam for gauge 1 by
Märklin, *circa 1913*. (Whereas the leading pony truck
wheels are correct, the truck frames do not correspond to
the original.) Torry Collection

6 A gauge 1, live steam, 'Great Bear' by Märklin, *circa 1909*.
In relative terms, the steam version would appear to be
the more common of the three types illustrated.
Torry Collection

1

2

1 An interesting picture of Märklin's LSWR 4–6–0 'Paddle Box' in clockwork for gauge 1, *circa 1910,* arriving at an English-styled station by Märklin bearing the name 'Probstzella'. (Since World War II Probstzella has become a border city between East Germany and the Federal Republic.)   A. Bommer Collection

2 One of the largest six-coupled, live steam locomotives by Bing was modelled in the form of this Great Western 'Saint' Class locomotive bearing the name 'Saint George', for gauge 2, *circa 1912.* The gauge 1 version of this locomotive, which does not appear to have been catalogued until 1924 (strange in view of the fact that its 'sister' engine the LNWR 'Claughton' was first introduced in 1914), was in the form of 'Titley Court'. Great Western clerestory coaches by Carette, *circa 1907.*
(For Bassett-Lowke)

3 An extremely rare model by Carette, in gauge 1, of the SECR steam railcar. The drive in this little steam engine was by means of an oscillating cylinder mounted in the cab. The coach unit, see engraving, was also marketed as a self-propelled unit in steam or electric, although no prototype of such a vehicle existed on the SECR. *Circa 1908.*
(For Bassett-Lowke)   Torry Collection

1 Another superb interpretation by Bing of a British locomotive, this time a Great Central 'Sir Sam Fay' for clockwork, in gauge 1, *circa 1914*. The Great Central coaches were constructed from Jubb components. The Great Central 4–4–0 and tender named 'Sir Alexander' in clockwork, for gauge 1, *circa 1904*, illustrated, was produced in conjunction with a series of twelve-windowed clerestory coaches as a prize in a competition sponsored by the Great Central Railway. These coaches were not produced by Bing in their subsequent series.
(For Bassett-Lowke)   Torry Collection

2 A contrast in gauge 1 clockwork 'Atlantics': at left, the Great Northern version by Bing (also fashioned in steam and electric), *circa 1907*, at right, the Märklin version (which in some way resembled the small boilered prototype), in the later London North Eastern livery. The original Märklin 'Atlantics' of this type were introduced in 1911. Although the prototypes on which these models may have been based were somewhat different, the picture clearly illustrates the variance in approach of two manufacturers. The Bing model is undoubtedly superior in appearance and authenticity of livery. In pure 'collecting' terms, however, rather more subjective considerations prevail. Water tower by Carette.
(Bing 'Atlantic' for Bassett-Lowke)

4 Part of a showcase at Bassett-Lowke's High Holborn shop just before World War 1.

3 A Bing Lancashire and Yorkshire, clockwork, 'Hughes' 4–6–0 and tender in gauge 1, *circa 1912*, somewhat untypically heads a goods train comprising private owner wagons by Carette, *circa 1909*.
(For Bassett-Lowke)

5 A superlative clockwork 'Wainwright E' in gauge 1, by Bing, *circa 1913*.
(For Bassett-Lowke)   Torry Collection

1

2

2 A North Eastern 0–4–4 'Class 0' Tank locomotive (in foreground) in clockwork by Bing, *circa 1914*, together with a London and South Western 'M7' 0–4–4 Tank in clockwork by Bing, *circa 1909*, LSWR full brake by Carette, *circa 1908*. All items for gauge 1.
(*For Bassett-Lowke*)   Torry Collection

3

1 Uncatalogued model of a Caledonian Railway 'Cardean' in clockwork for gauge 1, *circa 1914*. This magnificent example of Märklin's work borders on scale representation, but nonetheless, it retains certain Märklin features such as the driving wheels not recessing sufficiently into the splashers. This is an exceedingly rare model and little contemporary evidence of its existence has so far been discovered. One explanation is that it was produced as part of a special order for a Scottish store and not revived after 1918.

3 One of the largest and heaviest 2½″ gauge steam locomotives by Carette, *circa 1905*, was modelled on a North Eastern Railway 'Smith Compound'. Also illustrated is a Carette NER coach, *circa 1908*.
(*For Bassett-Lowke*)   Torry Collection

1 Gauge 1 Märklin 'George V' supplied exclusively to Gamage. W. E. Finlason writes: 'This LNWR inside-cylinder live steam 4–4–0 and a similar Midland model, were advertised in the Gamage Christmas Bazaar Catalogue of 1913. They would seem to have been marketed only through this outlet and at this time. They were two-cylinder models and there was no extant Märklin hardware which was quite adaptable to the requirement. The solution adopted was unique. Two ordinary outside cylinder assemblies together with their valve chests were mounted inside the frames. This left no room for the traditional steam reversing block – but why stick to tradition? Märklin's made the two-cylinder engine unit drive an auxiliary crankshaft, whilst the drive from that crankshaft, to the leading pair of driving wheels was via a reversing gear cluster, such as is fitted as standard to clockwork locomotives! But surely slip-eccentric reversing would have been cheaper and simpler? Yes, it would, but then one would not have had the reversing lever in the cab, which in those days was a selling point. The methylated spirit feed from the tender was also unique and passed via a large-diameter inverted U-tube to the burner in the firebox. The successful working of this device was very dependent on the correct wick being threaded into the U-tube. The whole length of the loco frames, running plate and splashers was a single piece of cast iron, a practice favoured by Märklin's for several of their gauge 1 live steam locomotives at this period.'

2

3

2 An LNWR Webb 'Cauliflower' 0–6–0 locomotive and tender, clockwork for gauge 0 by Bing, *circa 1912*. Rolling stock includes an assortment of Carette and Bing wagons, in particular, the Carette boiler wagon, *circa 1909*, advertising W. J. Bassett-Lowke's original family business in Northampton. (The boiler wagon, together with certain other Carette lithographed goods stock, continued in production at Winteringham's after 1920.)
(For Bassett-Lowke)

3 A derailment later in the day gives us the opportunity of seeing the unique final drive system adopted by Märklin for its Gamage 'George V' gauge 1, live steam model (see fig. 1).

1

1 An early Continental four-wheel car giving equal space to smokers and abstainers, thought to be by Märklin, for gauge 1, *circa 1909*.

O. Baur Collection

2

2 A further variation of Märklin's primitive coaches for gauge 0, *circa 1900*.

3

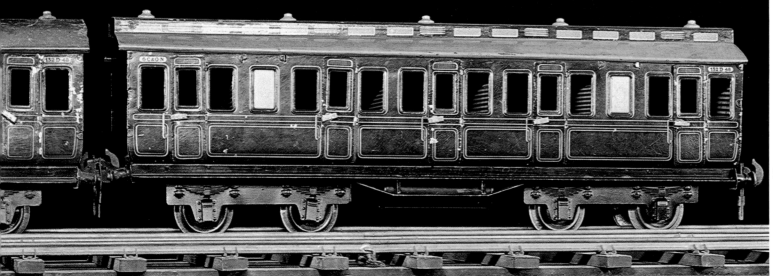

3 This gauge 1 clerestory coach by Carette, *circa 1907*, is something of an oddity. A strange grey livery has been applied to a standard GWR coach, presumably to satisfy Continental tastes. The coach partly shown also displays a freelance livery, once again applied to a standard Carette LNWR coach, *circa 1909*.

Torry Collection

4

5

6

7

4 A beautiful Märklin 53 cm '1st Class' PLM car for
gauge 1, originally introduced in 1919, but here, as in
fig. 6, with round roof as fitted in 1929.
A. Bommer Collection

5 An extremely rare blue and white 53 cm CIWL car
(probably made to special order) by Märklin for gauge 1,
circa 1920. A. Bommer Collection

6 A simulated wood finish 53 cm CIWL 'Sleeping Car' by
Märklin for gauge 1, *circa 1919.* A. Bommer Collection

7 On the basis that all is yet to be revealed, this remarkably
accurate 'Est' clockwork 4–6–0 and tender in gauge 1,
attributed to Bing, might for the moment be considered
to be the genuine article. The dual coloured 'Est' car is
certainly the work of Bing – or is it? Perhaps they were
trade samples for the French market in the pre-1914
period.
Photo Nauroy Studios Count Giansanti Collection

8 Bing gauge 4 'Gepackwagen', *circa 1912.*

8

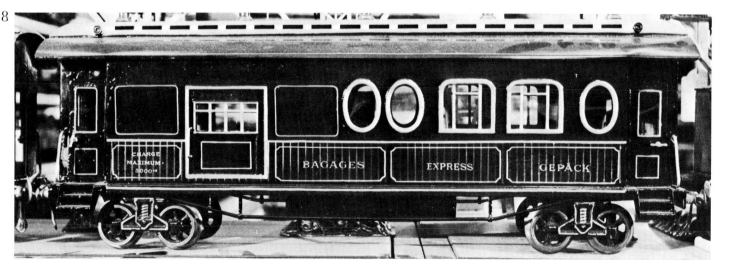

1 Gauge 3 'Atlantic' in live steam by Märklin, *circa 1913*. This generation of locomotives was the last in this gauge. It is unlikely that they were a great commercial success, and those catalogued after the first world war were almost certainly pre-war stock. (See page 176 for an interesting English variation of this locomotive.)
Photo Nauroy Studios   Count Giansanti Collection

2 Bing gauge 4 ($2\frac{15}{16}''$) live steam 'Atlantic' and tender shown with Bing's coaches for this gauge, *circa 1912*. (For detail of the first coach see fig. 8, page 75.) These items were shot *in situ* at Dr. Bommer's remarkable collection in Zurich. (Note one of the first gauge 3 Märklin clockwork locomotives of 1891 in centre of showcase.)

3 Count Giansanti's celebrated live steam 4–4–0 and tender, *circa 1912*, was the largest locomotive made for gauge 3 by Märklin. This particular example was extensively restored by the Italian firm of Elettren.
Photo Nauroy Studios   Count Giansanti Collection

4

4 Märklin's PLM 'Pacifics' for gauge 1, first introduced in 1912, were one of their longest running 'foreign' prototypes. The example illustrated is a steam version, heading a train of 53 cm PLM cars, *circa 1919*. An extremely attractive pull-out illustration, in colour, of the complete Märklin PLM train was issued with the firm's French catalogue in 1925.　　　A. Bommer Collection

5 An electric version of the gauge 1 Märklin PLM 'Pacific' (produced until 1929), this time heading a 53 cm CIWL blue car introduced with the prototypes in 1922.
　　　A. Bommer Collection

5

1

1 At left, a Bing live steam, 4–4–4 'Windcutter' at the head of a Bing 48·5 cm car, at right, a Bing electric 'Pacific'. All items for gauge 1, *circa 1912*.

R. McCrindell Collection

2

2 An extremely rare and uncatalogued, live steam 'Pacific' for gauge 1. The first vehicle of the train is an unusual 'penitentiary' car for France by Märklin, *circa 1905*. The locomotive is ascribed to Märklin, but in view of its obscurity, no date can be assigned to it.

Count Giansanti Collection

3 In 1929 Bassett-Lowke constructed this life-size replica in wood and cardboard of the 'Royal Scot' smokebox in order to launch its own gauge 0 version of that locomotive. I doubt if latter-day model train manufacturers have ever managed anything quite so flamboyant. This approach is a reflection of W. J. Bassett-Lowke's concern for design and style in the company's advertising and promotion.
Photo R. Fuller Collection

THE DIFFICULT MIDDLE YEARS

In the world of model railways, the years between the great wars were notable for the rise of Frank Hornby's business in both England and France. Hornby were to become one of the last major manufacturers of gauge 0 model railway equipment, and it is certain that their system was the most complete on the English market. It is doubtful whether any commercial firm in Europe achieved the excellence of Hornby's customer relations, and 'Meccano Magazine' was probably one of the best 'House' magazines ever published.

Bassett-Lowke in association with Winteringham Limited (Bassett-Lowke's independent but associated manufacturing arm in Northampton) also marketed more wholly British manufactured items, in particular, the long running 'Mogul' series, introduced in 1926.

A BOY'S PARADISE

Märklin continued to lead the field in Europe, and while gauge 1 and the larger gauges were in steady decline, their gauge 0 range was brought to a peak during the 1930's, culminating in a series of large express locomotives. The last development may have been caused by Robert Marescot's production of more accurate model railways in Paris from 1927 onwards, since his firm set new standards in one of Märklin's traditional markets. In terms of mass-production, Marescot's 'Etat' Pacific is still considered to be a masterpiece, and this standard was maintained by J. Fournereau, who acquired Marescot's production in 1928 and beyond to the creation of Munier semi-scale engines and rolling stock after the second world war. Reflecting these developments were Märklin's superb 1930 catalogues, which included the unforgettable reproductions of paintings by Josef Danilowatz.

At the beginning of the 1930's, Märklin, assuming the mantle of the now defunct Bing, collaborated with Bassett-Lowke to produce what were to be the last Anglo-German gauge 0 locomotives. This series comprised four models exclusive to Bassett-Lowke: a GWR 'King' Class, an LMS '5XP', a 2–6–4 LMS Tank and an SR 'Schools' Class. At first these models were supplied as completed engines and later (when Winteringham had overcome the problems with the then new 'Permag' mechanism) as bodywork only. In the USA, Lionel were to complete the absorption of Ives by 1931, and with American Flyer were to dominate the American market for the rest of this period. American Flyer were absorbed into the A. C. Gilbert Company in 1938, and both names were later to become synonymous with S gauge. Dorfan trains enjoyed a brief popularity. Their adherence to a unique diecast body assembly for their locomotives, coupled with a limited commercial existence, ensured that Dorfan trains would eventually become greatly sought after by collectors. Contemporary customers, however, had less foresight, as the Forcheimer Brothers, who founded Dorfan in 1920, found to their cost.

During the 1920's and 1930's the seeds of a common phenomenon were sown in the USA and Europe. The products of Ives in America were extended a reverence that anybody who had not undergone the American experience found it hard to understand, and the cult of Hornby in Britain and Märklin in

3

Europe assumed comparable proportions. The reason for the phenomenon probably lies in the fact that the products of these manufacturers touched an unprecedented range of personal experience, and the Ives, Hornby and Märklin generations were the first to sustain into adulthood their fierce loyalties to a purely mass-produced article. The fading of personal nostalgia may well bring a more objective assessment of the relative merits of these products, but it cannot diminish their makers' importance. H0 and 00 scales began to find their place towards the latter part of the 1930's, after the false dawns heralded by Schoenner in 1902 and by Bing's table railway system in 1922. Märklin had established a very complete three-rail H0 system by the late thirties, Stefan Bing's son Franz in association with Stefan Kahn, encouraged by Bassett-Lowke, commenced the Trix Express H0 Line in Germany in 1935, and in 1938 Hornby launched the first two sets of its 'Dublo' series in clockwork and three-rail electric. Then in 1939, all the signals once again registered stop. Nothing, not even model trains, was to be quite the same afterwards. Although tinplate and metal diecast model trains would linger on for a while, the mass market (with one or two notable exceptions) was to be dominated in the ensuing era by new super-detailed plastic.

5 Notwithstanding the flanged wheels, this toy floor train, loosely styled on the rebuilt Metropolitan Railway electric locomotive, also incorporated bogies that were capable of being pre-set (track width $2\frac{3}{4}''$), thought to be by 'Eha' Toys, *circa 1922*. Torry Collection

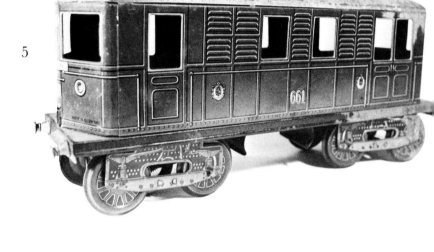

5

1 Introduction to the last Stevens's Model Dockyard catalogue in 1926, with an accompanying notice informing patrons of the expiration of their lease.

1

2 Listed by Schoenner in 1905, this flash-back to one of the first trackless floor locomotives, based on a contemporary prototype, is probably the finest example of this *genre* ever made. It was produced in three sizes, the example illustrated being the largest, with a track width of $3\frac{1}{2}''$

2

3   Bing's things for the floor! On the left, a directional floor train, *circa 1922*, using components normally found on regular models, the front driving wheels having the facility to be set on either a right or left hand lock; the cars had similar interlocking for running in circles. (Track width 1¼".) The little locomotive on the right is typical of Bing's cheap range of floor trains which originated in the pre-1914 period (track width 1¾").

4   A little clockwork floor engine by Oro, incorporating a delayed reverse mechanism operated by the large gear visible between the main wheels. (Track width 2", *circa* 1925.)

1

ENGLISH-MADE ELECTRIC LOCOMOTIVE AND TENDER.

(As illustration), to run on 4-v accumulator, will pull 7⅛ lb., beautifully enamelled in correct colours of the L.N.E.R. & L.M.S. Railway. 17 ins. long. Post free. Price **37/6**

1 It does not necessarily take an exotic train to make an interesting picture. The Bowman 0–4–0 gauge 0, live steam, Tank, *circa 1928*, about to clear the 'Brimtoy Bridge', heading a Bowman Great Western coach with opening doors and all, is a typical example of that firm's products which can best be described as honest, durable, efficient and incredibly ugly. Bowman of Norwich commenced his business in the late 1920's by producing steam engines designed to power Meccano models. The firm ceased business in the mid 1930's.

ENGLISH-MADE ELECTRIC TANK LOCOMOTIVE. (As illustration).

Enamelled in the correct colours of the L.N.E.R. & L.M.S. Railway runs on 4—6 volts and will pull a load of 7½ lbs. 12¼ ins. long. Price **52/6** Post free.

2 A selection of Bar Knight locomotives as advertised in the 1924 Gamage catalogue. This obscure little firm, based in Scotland, produced some very simple and exceptionally crude locomotives. The star of the line was a 4–4–4 Tank locomotive which was almost a parody of the beautiful Glasgow & South Western 'Baltic' prototype.

ENGLISH-MADE GAUGE 0-1⅛-in. ELECTRIC TANK LOCO.

(As illustration), beautifully finished in correct colours of L.M.S. & L.N.E.R. Will pull a load of 7 lbs. running from a 4-volt accumulator. Length 9 ins. Price **22/6** Post free.

ENGLISH-MADE MODEL OF L.M.S. RAILWAY PILOT LOCOMOTIVE.

Gauge 0. Length over all, 6⅛ ins. Diameter of boiler, 1⅜ ins. Brass boiler with steam safety valve, funnel, etc. Pair brass tube oscillating cylinders and piston rods. Engine enamelled and lined in L.M.S. colours, mounted on four cast flanged locomotive wheels. Complete with lamp, measure, filler, and full directions, as illustrated. Gauge 0=1⅛ in. Price **12/6** Post 6d.

Note.—The above engine travels under its own steam a quarter of a mile.

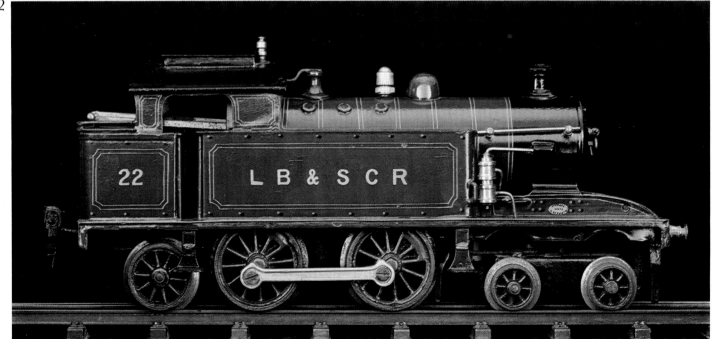

1 An extremely rare LNWR 'Bowen-Cooke' 4–6–2 Tank, in gauge 0 clockwork, by Märklin, *circa 1913*. A gauge 1 version of this locomotive was produced by that firm in both LNWR and LMS liveries. This type was also available in gauge 2 by Bing.

3 Original LBSCR-liveried version of the Märklin gauge 0 clockwork 'Baltic Tank', *circa 1921*. This particular model was also turned out in an all-black livery, presumably for the Continental market, and in a freelance LMS red. (According to Bonds' catalogue of 1934 an LNER-liveried version was also available.)

4 A Southern-liveried version of an ex-LBSCR 'Baltic Tank' in gauge 0, clockwork, *circa 1923*, by Märklin. These models are more popularly known as 'Stephensons'. Märklin neither produced LBSCR nor Southern coaches for this locomotive, and the brown and white Pullman series (see fig. 6, page 109) were the nearest contemporary rolling stock in the mid-1920 range. The six-coupled mechanism fitted to this model was adapted and used in a series of controlled clockwork Tank engines marketed by an obscure British firm known as Walker-Fenn.

2 A charming LBSCR gauge 0, clockwork, Tank by Märklin, *circa 1920*. I think this model illustrates the naivety referred to in the introduction, not quite a scale model, yet not quite a toy.

3

4

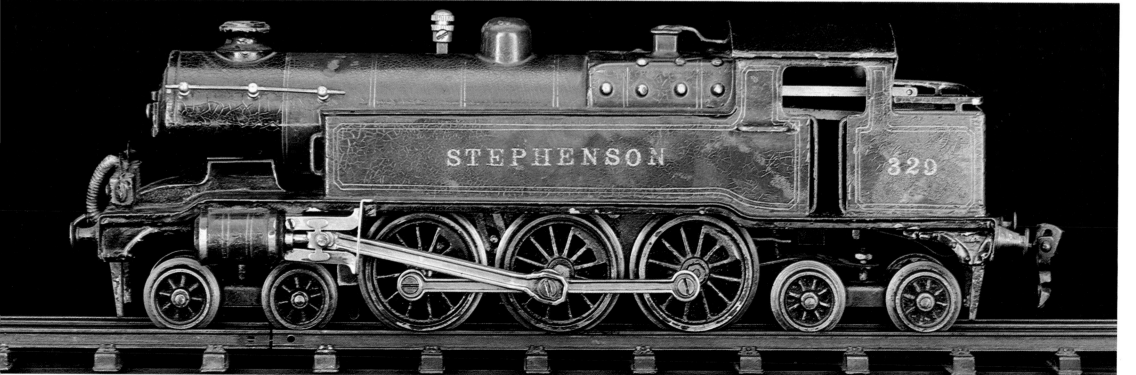

1 The prototype of this 0 gauge Märklin clockwork
locomotive was known as a 'Flatiron'. Because of its long
wheelbase, this model required a 2–4–4 wheel
configuration for running on tight curves, instead of the
0–6–4 wheel arrangement of the prototype. (*Circa 1913.*)
(This is an example of a model taken from an earlier
period and grouped with its immediate successors. See
also page 84, fig. 1.)

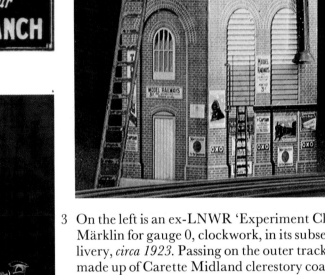

3 On the left is an ex-LNWR 'Experiment Class' by
Märklin for gauge 0, clockwork, in its subsequent LMS
livery, *circa 1923*. Passing on the outer track is a train
made up of Carette Midland clerestory coaches, *circa 1909*,
hauled by a Bing Midland 'Single' in clockwork – one of
the few scale-proportioned 'Singles' ever produced in
gauge 0, *circa 1913*, and as such, greatly sought after.
Both these locomotives were made principally for
Gamage, although the Midland 'Single' was offered by
Bassett-Lowke for a short time.

2 Märklin's gauge 0 clockwork version of an ex-LNWR
'Precursor' Tank in LMS livery, *circa 1923*.

4 Gauge 1, clockwork, ex-Great Northern 'N1' Tank by Bing, which has undergone a post-grouping Bassett-Lowke repaint, in order to display the standard black LNER Tank livery, *circa 1923*. The original Bing 'N1's' were introduced *circa 1912*, in both gauge 1 and gauge 2. This model was unquestionably one of the very best scale representations of this period. Also illustrated are 1921-series Bing LNER teak coaches and a Märklin brake van for Gamage, *circa 1911*.
(For Bassett-Lowke)

5 Although the extremely popular 4–4–2 'Precursor' Tank by Bing was introduced before the first world war, it was still marketed by Bassett-Lowke well into the mid-1920's. This version, in gauge 0 clockwork, heads a rake of 1921-series LNWR coaches by Bing.

3 There is some evidence to suggest that about twenty gauge 1, non stream-lined 'Hudsons' by Märklin, in electric, were supplied to America in the mid 1930's. A magnificent original example is illustrated, although the tender was not available at the time of photography.
Photo Bommer   A. Bommer Collection

1 American Flyer was the only American manufacturer to attempt a model of a European type, although the Ives factory records also show a British-type cast iron clockwork locomotive. (It is not known if this item was actually put into production.) Illustrated is an example marketed as 'British Flyer' comprising a cast-iron-bodied 'GNR Tank' in clockwork for gauge 0, with a tender – presumably for good measure – and two GNR lithographed tinplate coaches, *circa 1920*. An LNWR 'George V' type 0–4–0 and tender was also marketed in this way. It is amusing to reflect on the copy used in a contemporary Gamage advertisement describing these products: 'The most perfect and powerful miniature rolling stock in the world. Fine, strong, British models, on British lines, right up to date.'

2 An interesting factory adaptation of the gauge 1 bodywork of a 4–4–4 electric type by Bing for gauge 0, *circa 1926*. This locomotive normally appeared in Canadian Pacific maroon, but the example depicted, together with complementary cars, is in the extremely rare, vivid orange livery of the Chicago/Milwaukee and St. Paul. (Around 1912 Ives also marketed their gauge 1 car bodies on gauge 0 trucks.)   A. Bommer Collection

2

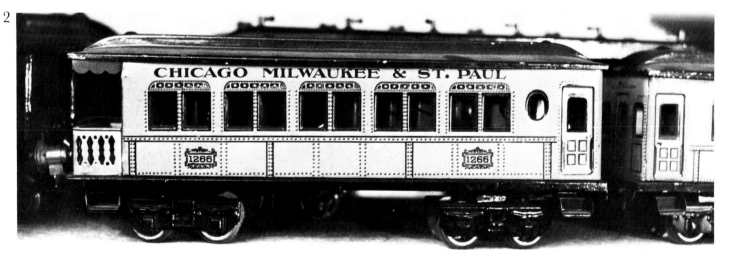

3

5

4

WASHINGTON EXPRESS
EXACTLY AS ILLUSTRATED ABOVE
Locomotive, Tender, Combination Car, Day Coach, Pullman Car and Observation Car.
Length Overall 9 ft. 2½ in.   Oval Track 80″ wide by 122″ long
We recommend a transformer of 150 watt capacity.   Locomotive equipped with Two double field motors and Remote Control.   Price—complete $98.00 F. O. B. New York.

4 Boucher held themselves to be one of the superior
American manufacturers, and it is generally recognised
that their products possessed a special kind of quality.
The 2⅛″ gauge 'Washington Express' illustrated across the
centre spread of their 1929 catalogue was not in fact
marketed in that form, and the coaches illustrated were
'mock-ups' utilising American Flyer components. Boucher
also made an excellent range of model launches, but
perhaps their products were too superior, for they did not
survive the ravages of the 1930s, although I understand
that the company is still in existence.

5 Boucher were the exclusive importers of Bassett-Lowke's
Greenly designed, gauge 1, live steam, American 'Pacific'
and, in fact, marketed this locomotive in the USA as
'Boucher' in the early 1920's. The model illustrated
purports to be an example of the Greenly design, but
further investigation suggests that this is probably a
locomotive built to similar designs by L. Lawrence
('LBSC'), who named this particular design the 'Ford'
Pacific. There was intense rivalry between Henry Greenly
and 'LBSC', and the latter designed his American gauge 1
'Pacific' locomotive in 1925 as a direct challenge to
Greenly's virtually unrivalled position as a consultant
designer to the model locomotive trade. 'LBSC's'
drawings and castings for this 'Pacific' were available
through the British firm of Kennions.
Photo Udel Studios   E. Hoffman Collection

1

1 At left, Lionel's electric gauge 0 Union Pacific 'City of Portland', three-car diesel unit, *circa 1934* (see front section of silver version, page 113) alongside a Mini Scale NYC 'Hudson', *circa 1937*, for gauge 0, also electric powered. Both locomotives are overshadowed by Lionel's famous 'Hell Gate Bridge', which was, in fact, designed for single track running. The Mini Scale locomotive was available in kit form, and like so many American locomotives, it was at that time constructed from castings which made it incredibly heavy.

NYC 'Hudson' – Torry Collection

3 Superb electric, non stream-lined 'Hudson' by Märklin, *circa 1934*. The majority of these locomotives were produced with silver-painted smokeboxes. The twelve-wheel Pullman car is probably the finest 0 gauge representation of an American car by a European manufacturer, and it was only, in fact, listed by Märklin in their USA catalogue. (The Louis Hertz collection contains some remarkable variations of this Hudson as follows:–

i The original factory sample finished in a striking brown livery.

ii A live-steam version finished in white for a customer who believed this livery accorded with the Kaiser's 'special' locomotive.

iii Other variations include a gloss and matt finish, and the earlier version as illustrated on page 92 (fig. 1) with an 8″ tender as distinct from the $8\frac{5}{8}$″ tender of the final version.)

2 Ives electric locomotive for gauge 0, *circa 1932*, with a mix of Lionel and Ives cars. These cars are sometimes erroneously referred to as 'Transition Ives'. In fact, the Ives 'Transition' period relates to Ives products manufactured between 1928 and 1930, during which time the company was under the joint proprietorship of American Flyer, Hafner and Lionel. Grand Central Station by Lionel. At right a stamped tin-bodied '3200' series Ives electric locomotive, *circa 1919*.

2

3

4 A gauge 0 electric, 'Commodore Vanderbilt', *circa 1935,* is basically the stream-lined version of the 'Hudson' illustrated in fig. 3. This locomotive was the American representative in the famous Märklin quartet of mid 1930 gauge 0 express locomotives.
Count Giansanti Collection

4

5 A gauge 1 electric version of the 'Commodore Vanderbilt' by Märklin, *circa 1936,* which differs wholly in construction from its gauge 0 counterpart. Considerable mystery surrounds some of Märklin's gauge 1 products of the mid 1930's, and it is thought that this engine was available to special order for it bears signs of hand fabrication, albeit at Märklin's factory. Also illustrated is a rare Märklin Pullman car bearing the name 'Louisiana', *circa 1920.* Count Giansanti Collection

5

1 The original 'simple' non-catalogued Märklin gauge 0, electric, NYC 'Hudson' *circa 1933.* See page 91, fig. 3 for final version.
Photo Nauroy Studios   Count Giansanti Collection

2 A gauge 0 Bing 'Pacific' in electric, illustrates the simplest approach to the Americanisation of a standard model, in this instance the mere addition of a cow catcher and electric light. This item does not appear to have been catalogued, although the German version was introduced in 1927/8.   A. Bommer Collection

3 There is a strong fascination surrounding things that might have been. Of this prototype sample locomotive illustrated below Harold Carstens writes: 'This giant Lionel Super 381 was never put into production, but it was displayed for thirty years at the firm's showroom.' (The example illustrated is one of two prototypes made in Italy.)
Photograph by courtesy of Carstens Publications Inc.

5

4 Dorfan's famous 'take-apart' locomotive as listed in the 1930 catalogue, for 'wide' gauge. This manufacturer was one of the first to use high pressure diecastings, and the size of some of these early castings gave rise to a tendency to warping with all its associated problems.

5 A Lionel standard-gauge (2⅛″ gauge) '385E' 2–4–2 in electric, *circa 1933*, with three 'Stephen Girard' cars. These cars formed Lionel's '424' series which were named 'Liberty Bell', 'Stephen Girard' and 'Coral Isle'. *Circa 1930.* A. Bommer Collection

6

6 Weedon parts were utilised by the Steam Electric Company of Blomfield, New Jersey to produce this extraordinary 0 gauge steam locomotive, fired on an immersion heater system with power for the heater element being picked up from the track (locomotive reversed to show heater element). Final drive is via gears driven by twin oscillating cylinders. This locomotive which was virtually the last attempt by an American manufacturer to produce an 0 gauge, live steam locomotive was produced to couple with the Lionel tender as illustrated. *Circa 1930.*
Photo Udel Studios E. Hoffman Collection

7 One of the only model locomotives produced by the A. C. Gilbert Company prior to their acquisition of American Flyer in 1938, was this 2½″ gauge New York Central 'Hudson' type built from an 'Erector' construction set of the early 1930's. An electric motor was available for this model, but only to turn the motion for display purposes, and it was primarily a 'push-along' locomotive. It is interesting to note that 'Buddy L' (Moline Pressed Steel Company, Illinois) also produced large motorless trains of scale proportions for 2″ and 3¼″ gauges, during the 1920's and early 1930's, and this type of large scale metal train was virtually unique to North America.

7

1   Märklin's 'NL 13000' series, three-car set in electric for gauge 0, *circa 1929* (see fig. 6, page 109).
                    Count Giansanti Collection

2   'Berliner Untergrundbahn' of 1927, gauge 0 electric, which utilises the basic bodies manufactured by Bing at that time for its 'Mitropa' cars, as well as for a variety of British liveried vehicles.
                    Count Giansanti Collection

3   Bing Metropolitan Railway three-car electric set in rare maroon and cream livery, gauge 0, *circa 1927*. Further Bing versions of these sets utilised LNER teak lithographed cars of a similar pattern.
                    Count Giansanti Collection

5

4 In the USA the 1930s evidenced the overwhelming popularity of electric toy trains, even to the point where electric outline types were more popular than the historically more glamorous 'steamers'. Quite the reverse could be said of Europe. Typical of these trains was Lionel's standard gauge range well illustrated by this head-on view of their famous '402' locomotive.

5 Although one would not have thought that model trains had reached the stage when they would attract forgeries, I have during my travels, encountered some very unusual items, mostly purporting to be Märklin. I know of a superbly faked pair of Plank hot-air trams that float (presumably on their own hot air!) around the auction rooms and collections of Europe. I am simply not certain that this uncatalogued, and as far as one can ascertain, unique two-car Netherland set in electric, for gauge 1, bearing all the hallmarks of Märklin, comes into the above category, but nonetheless, an air of mystery inevitably surrounds such items. One theory is that it was

made by Märklin apprentices, another, that it was a partly complete trade sample which has subsequently been given motive power. The latter theory is given some credibility by the fact that the bodies appear to be authentic, although little of Märklin's traditional methods are apparent in the fabrication of the bogie structures. No date is offered.

O. Baur Collection

1

1 Twin Streetcar set by Märklin, produced in either green and white, all white, or blue and white as illustrated. The latter versions were assumed to be based on the Munich and Zurich Streetcar systems. The well-used model illustrated is in clockwork for gauge 0, *circa 1928*. (Note: The frames appear to have been cut away on the motorised car.)   A. Bommer Collection

2

2 A superb example of a classic 'collectors' item' is the gauge 1, electric 'Rheinuferbahn' by Märklin, *circa 1929*. (A two-car set is illustrated.) The model was not a great commercial success when first introduced, but unlike some models which become supreme collectors' pieces by virtue of rarity alone, (normally arising as a result of commercial failure) this elegant model has achieved a pre-eminence in its own right and represents the ultimate development of Märklin's tinplate 'Inter-Urban' trains.
Photo Lewis Studios   M. Roberts Collection

3 The Bing for Bassett-Lowke series of coaches, generally known as the '1921-series', included the pre-grouping liveries introduced in 1921 and 1922, and the post-grouping liveries introduced in the late twenties. Illustrated is a 1921-series, Bing, Great Western 3rd Brake, available only for gauge 0 in this livery, *circa 1928.* *(For Bassett-Lowke)* Torry Collection

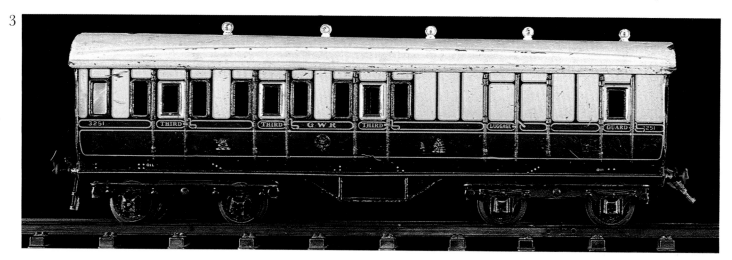

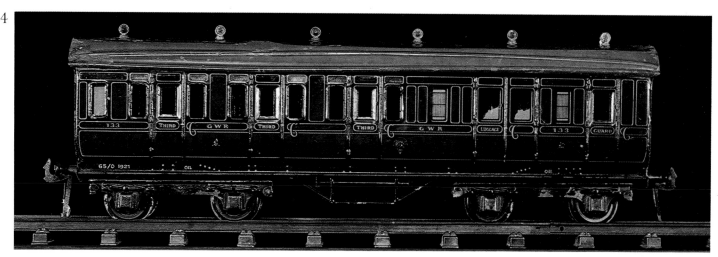

4 A gauge 0, Bing, Great Western 3rd Brake coach, *circa 1921*, in the rare 'Lake' livery adopted by the Great Western Railway during the period 1911–1922. *(For Bassett-Lowke)*

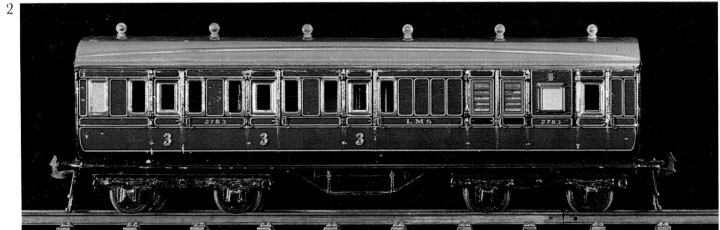

1 The rarest of all Bing 1921-series coaches marketed by Bassett-Lowke, were the second series, post-grouping coaches in Southern Railway livery. The coach illustrated, *circa 1926*, is an original lithographed version in gauge 0. Originally Southern coaches were merely GWR Lake-liveried stock, overpainted by hand, used to supply passenger stock in Southern Railway livery.
(For Bassett-Lowke)   Torry Collection

2 Bing, gauge 0, LMS 3rd Brake coach, *circa 1925*.
(For Bassett-Lowke)

3 Bing, gauge 0, LNER teak, 3rd Brake coach, *circa 1926*.
(For Bassett-Lowke)   Torry Collection

4 Bing repeated some of its pre-first-world-war range for Bassett-Lowke in the post-1918 period, and the 'King Arthur', live steam, gauge 1 locomotive, *circa 1923*, is an excellent example of the up-dating of the earlier LSWR liveried 'Urie' 4–6–0. Another notable example was the continuation of the production of LNWR 'Claughtons' first introduced in 1914, some of which were offered in LMS livery during the mid 1920's.

(For Bassett-Lowke)   Count Giansanti Collection

5 Fathers had to raise a lot of smoke before their sons could apply for one of these locomotives! It is interesting to note how in the late 1920's Bing's trade mark featured prominently on its British products, whereas in earlier years they were in the main discreetly hidden under tenders, or even painted out.

6 Märklin's interpretation of a Southern Railway 'Lord Nelson' for gauge 1, live steam, *circa 1927*. Once again this model depicts Märklin's almost total disregard for the proportions of the prototype. It is interesting to compare this Southern Railway locomotive with that of Bing's 'King Arthur', illustrated with a similar Märklin Pullman coach, in fig. 4.   A. Bommer Collection

5

Model Railways FREE

Every boy can have his own railway—be his own Station Master or Engineer by collecting B.D.V. Coupons

The first 2,000 Boys to send for a Free Engine will also be presented with a Tender

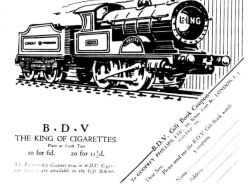

4

6

1 An interesting example of a Carette design produced at Winteringham's from the original tooling which was sent over from Germany after the cessation of Carette's business in 1917. The 0–4–0 locomotive is in gauge 0, live steam, and the short clerestory coach was by Märklin with LMS overprinting on the original Midland Railway designation, *circa 1923*. (An almost identical 0–4–0 locomotive in LNWR livery was offered by the London firm of F. Henschel & Co., in 1914.)

2 A further example of relatively late primitive Märklin, *circa 1924*, which stretches credibility even further by having the LNER locomotive named 'George V', (in commercial terms as related to the toy trade, this particular name may have been justified). There are further examples of this particular model bearing the name 'Great Bear' (no LNER 'Pacific' bore this name either). The particular locomotive illustrated is in gauge 0, live steam, and heads a train comprising Märklin standard 40 cm Continental cars, finished as LNER teak coaches, *circa 1934*. Once again, the assumption must be that these coaches were to special order, which accords with the anomalous situation that there are more relatively unexplained Märklin production models dating from the 1930's than from the earlier, and presumably less well documented eras.   Count Giansanti Collection

3

4

4 'The Real Thing' – as Northampton phrased it when they issued the 'Mogul' series during the 1925/26 season.

3 The Northampton-made equivalent of Märklin's '5XP', *circa 1936,* (see fig. 5, page 115) in gauge 0 electric. The LMS 'Dining Saloon' by Exley is *circa 1935.*

5 An ex-Great Central 4–6–0 'City of London' fashioned by Stronlite of Japan on the Leeds 'Sir Sam Fay' model. Gauge 0, electric, *circa 1930.* In the author's view, the copy is every bit as good as the original. In this illustration, the beautiful Pullman coach is of all-metal construction, thought to have been produced as a prototype by Milbro. Locomotive restoration by Littledale.

5

1

1 A further example of Stronlite's obsession with Leeds products. A version of a gauge 0, electric, 'Saddle' Tank in Southern livery, *circa 1935*. Although designated 'Southern' the coaches, also by Stronlite, are of original design and make little pretence of being anything other than oriental. They did however excel themselves by producing lithographed tinplate versions of Leeds' paper-lithographed, wooden-bodied Pullman coaches.

3 Even Stronlite baulked at copying this very individual Leeds model of an LNER Sentinel Cammell steam railcar 'Nettle' in gauge 0 electric, *circa 1933*. The model was mainly constructed from wood and was 'wallpapered' with litho-coloured sheets.

2 An interesting picture of the great man himself, who apart from his many other interests was an extremely competent amateur photographer and cinematographer.

2   3

4

4 An 0 gauge electric 'Etat' Pacific describes a graceful curve at the head of its train. The locomotive and cars were manufactured briefly by Marescot, *circa 1928*, and this firm were to be the pioneers of authentic fine-scale trains.

Like so many pioneers, however, they were commercially ahead of their time. Marescot models were based on a scale of 23 millimetres to the metre.

M. Darphin Collection

6

5

5 A Delienne 'Etat' 0–6–0 electric Tank locomotive. Available as a ready-to-run model or as a set of castings, *circa 1935*, typical of many models that were available in France throughout the 1930s and in the post war period.

6 Another view of the superb Marescot 'Pacific' – offered in electric only – this version with smoke deflectors, *circa 1928*, was super-detailed by Fournereau. In the author's view, these items have in the past been most under-rated in collecting terms, and no doubt they will gain in importance as the dust – metaphorically – settles on this century of model trains.   Count Giansanti Collection

1

1 A selection of locomotives marketed by Louis Roussy under the name LR (Le Rapide) in France, during the 1930s. All these examples were for gauge 0 and possessed exceptionally low centres of gravity, which enabled them to support the claim that they were the 'fastest' model trains ever produced.

2 'Golden Arrow/Fleche d'Or' Nord Pacific for electric running by Jep in gauge 0, *circa 1930,* with a partial illustration of the superb lithographed Pullman cars by that firm.   Count Giansanti Collection

3 An even more interesting product of LR (Le Rapide) was this Michelin Railcar in clockwork, for gauge 0, *circa 1933.* The prototype was a special body fitted to a Hispano-Suiza chassis with Michelin-tyred wheels.

Count Giansanti Collection

4 On the far left a 'Nord' 4–4–4 by Jep pulls away from a Märklin canopied terminus, ahead of a Jep two-car diesel set. Both items are electric for gauge 0, *circa 1939*. The Jep range of gauge 0 locomotives were produced until the late 1950's.

5 A pair of gauge 0 electric engines by Doll, *circa 1930*. Doll manufactured railway products from 1918 to 1938, when they were absorbed by Gebr. Fleischmann. Their electric outline locomotives, while brightly coloured, were of very simple design, and by far and away the most important models of this little firm were their magnificent stationary engines, particularly their over-types.   Torry Collection

1 A typical electric, steam outline, 0 gauge train by the firm of Doll & Cie, produced throughout the 1930's, until that company's absorption into the firm of Gebr. Fleischmann (see fig. 4, page 173). All these trains bore a remarkable resemblance to the model trains of Kraus Fandor, another small German manufacturer of that time, whose products were highly regarded in the U.S.A., and in fact, were directly linked to the celebrated Dorfan company.
Torry Collection

2 Electric, gauge 0 'Atlantic', *circa 1928*, heading a train of wine-vat wagons, *circa 1930*. All items by Märklin.
Count Giansanti Collection

3 Products of Karl Bub have, in collecting terms, been treated rather like the 'poor relations', and perhaps this gauge 0 electric 'Pacific', *circa 1936*, which was one of the few attempts at prototype modelling by that firm, provides a reason for this lowly rating. (Compare this engine with its contemporary in the Märklin range – see fig. 2, page 116.) However, like so many things rarity has now subdued taste, and this particular item is greatly sought after by collectors. The 'Mitropa' car illustrated is by the same firm.
Count Giansanti Collection

4

4 This illustration of a Märklin electric, gauge 1 'Zeppelin' *circa 1936*, standing alongside a typical Märklin signal box of that time, tells us many things about the aesthetics of the 1930's. (Alfred B. Gottwaldts fascinating little book 'Schienenzeppelin' is highly recommended for further information on the prototype 'Schnell-Triebwagen' modelled by Märklin during the 1930's.)

Count Giansanti Collection

5 Little mystery surrounds this superb gauge 1, electric 'TK 66' Tank locomotive by Märklin, *circa 1936*. Both this and the 'HR 66' 'Pacific' in gauge 1 (see fig. 1, page 136) were produced in very small quantities, as they appeared at a time when gauge 1 had already reached the stage of rapid decline. The Wagon Déchargeur 'Talbot' also by Märklin, is an extreme rarity, *circa 1912*.

Count Giansanti Collection

5

1 A much better example of Bub's work is this 4 + 4 + 4 electric locomotive in gauge 0, *circa 1932*.
Count Giansanti Collection

2 The Märklin model of the gauge 0 electric Swiss 'Crocodile' was another legendary locomotive of the 1930's. This example, *circa 1933*, heads a train of Märklin 50 ton, 24.5cm mineral wagons.   M. Darphin Collection

3 A gauge 1 'Pacific' in live steam, by Märklin, at the head of a Märklin 53cm 'Gepäckwagen'. This light-weight gauge 1 'Pacific', *circa 1931*, was the last gauge 1 live steam locomotive produced by Märklin, and both this and the even rarer gauge 0 live steam version, were advertised as late as 1936/7.   Count Giansanti Collection

1

2

3

4 A gauge 1 version of the Märklin 'Crocodile', *circa 1933*, with assorted Märklin mineral and liquid cars. In the interests of negotiating standard curves, an axle was omitted from each electric power unit.

M. Darphin Collection

5

5 A mixture of manufacturers, illustrated by a little gauge 0 Doll BLS electric engine, taking charge of a train comprising Märklin's glamorous 'Golden Mountain' Pullman express cars, in the Montreux Bernese Oberland Railway livery, *circa 1931*. In reality, the prototype 'Golden Mountain' express lasted for only about four months, during the summer season of 1931.

M. Darphin Collection

6 This Märklin Pullman in gauge 0, *circa 1920,* is one of a series that was given the respective inscriptions, 'Alberta', 'Cleopatra', 'Car No. 4 Third Class' and 'Dining Saloon'. Variants of this basic 0 gauge body include the short-lived 'Golden Mountain Express' (fig. 5) for the Swiss market and the 'NL three-car electric set' for Holland (fig. 1, page 94).

Count Giansanti Collection

1 The beautiful German 'Pacific' for gauge 1 electric, *circa
   1928*, could be said to represent Bing's 'swansong' in
   prototype railway models. This particular model is
   extraordinarily light to handle, and totally different from
   the feel of earlier Bing, gauge 1, locomotives. The 48.5cm
   baggage car, illustrated, was based on the earlier 1912
   designs, which lasted until 1927.
                              Count Giansanti Collection

2 One of the last Bing designs of an International 'blue' car
   in gauge 0, *circa 1930*. This particular example was usually
   produced as a maroon 'Mitropa' car.   Torry Collection

3

3 Bing's penultimate model of a German 'Pacific' in gauge 0, clockwork, *circa 1927*, illustrated with Bing's 35 cm cars, *circa 1912*.

4 A '2–D–2' electric gauge 1 locomotive, *circa 1929*, for the Paris/Orleans Railway. This uncatalogued item is undoubtedly the largest electric type locomotive reputed to have been produced by Märklin, and up to date, only two examples are known to have come to light. Perhaps

the company had second thoughts about issuing this particular model in any quantity, or possibly they were built to special order, as was the practice with several gauge 1 types during the 1930's.   A. Bommer Collection

4

1 Märklin's version of a Swiss 'Ae 3/6' in electric, for gauge 0, heads a train of 'circus wagons', while below a train of special-load Märklin wagons awaits motive power. *Circa 1934.*   M. Darphin Collection

2 Completely unique in the 1930/40 Märklin range was this little 'Der Adler' set for gauge 0 electric, introduced in 1935. The model was produced to celebrate the Centenary of the Nuremburg Fürth Train. It is interesting to note that this little set, together with the 'Rocket' (see fig. 4, page 33) are virtually the only examples of pre-1870 prototypes attempted by Märklin. Clearly, it was still too early in the 1930's for the romantic appeal of the earliest railways to be turned to commercial advantage.

M. Darphin Collection

3 The final electric version of Märklin's 'Schnell-
Triebwagen', *circa 1937*, speeds over an embankment,
while below a train made up of Märklin mineral hoppers,
trundles behind a Märklin 'GR 66' locomotive, in
electric, *circa 1937*. (Both items for gauge 0.)
M. Darphin Collection

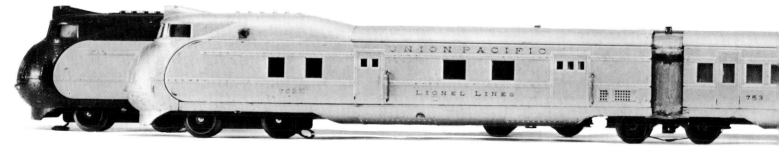

3

4 Named Tank wagons have always been popular, and
there appears to be an urge among collectors, to own
entire series of these vehicles, rather in the way that series
of private owners' vans and wagons are collected. This
picture depicts virtually all the gauge 0 tank cars issued by
Märklin in the mid-1930's, with the exception of the four-
wheel version of the 'BV Aral' car and the later four-wheel,
post-war, 'Esso' tank car.   M. Darphin Collection

4

1 Märklin's classic 40 cm restaurant car for the 'blue
train' in gauge 0.

2 Märklin gauge 0 at its zenith. A second-series 'Mountain
Etat', with 'full' Walschaerts valve gear, looms out of the
darkness with the 'blue train', *circa 1933*.

3 A 4–6–2 'Borsig' (prototype 4–6–4) gauge 0, electric, and tender by Märklin, *circa 1935*, hauls a train headed by a 40cm 'Mitropa' car. This locomotive formed part of the final series of Märklin gauge 0 express locomotives, which like their Hornby counterparts, were never revived after the second world war – although the standard German 'Pacific', not strictly speaking part of this series, appeared briefly in the post-war years. Historically, these Märklin products are of great importance in that they represent the pinnacle of mass-produced gauge 0 tinplate.

3

4

4 The 'Schools' Class locomotive, together with the '5XP', 'King George V' and 'LMS 2–6–4 Tank', comprised the series of the four gauge 0 locomotives referred to below. This particular example is one of the earlier batch fitted with original Märklin electric motor and valve gear, *circa 1933*. (Even when fitted with a British mechanism, the 'Schools' Class retained the original Märklin valve gear.) (*For Bassett-Lowke*)

5

5 A Märklin '5XP' for gauge 0, *circa 1935*. A beautiful example of one of the four Märklin locomotives prepared exclusively for Bassett-Lowke. As with Bing's work some twenty-five years previously, a German manufacturer has excelled in the production of an English outline model. The item illustrated is fitted with the British permag mechanism, and standard Bassett-Lowke Walschaerts valve gear. Also illustrated is one of a series of very elegant signals made by Märklin for the English market. (*For Bassett-Lowke*)   M. Darphin Collection

1 Train departures, in gauge 0, by Märklin in the mid 1930's. Left to right, three-car diesel unit in electric (a development of the twin-car 'Flying Hamburger' unit), 40cm CIWL Baggage car with curved 'International' roof, and a 4–6–4 'TK' Tank in electric at the head of two 40cm German cars. Experts may care to spot the anachronism in this picture.

4–6–4 'TK' Tank – Torry Collection

2 A life-long collector has stated that this electric locomotive, *circa 1929*, typified all that was best in Märklin's final gauge 0 production. A simple bold 'Pacific' design, coupled with the very fine, if not strictly scale, 40 cm Märklin range of mainline passenger cars, *circa 1934*. Examples of these 'Pacifics' appear after the second world war, when only the plain style of smoke deflector was used.

3 An all-black version of the 'Cock O' the North' in electric, for gauge 1, *circa 1936*, bearing the number '2001'. As with the 'Commodore Vanderbilt' illustrated on page 91, fig. 5, this gauge 1 locomotive ascribed to Märklin was not officially catalogued. However, as a greater number of pressed parts appear to have been used in its construction, it may represent a serious attempt to produce this model in quantity. There is a strong possibility that this was a partly finished prototype, completed after Märklin had ceased gauge 1 production in the late 1930's. (For a complete answer to this particular problem, a close comparison between the locomotive illustrated and that of Biaggi's post-war production 'Cock O' the Norths', might prove fruitful.)   A. Bommer Collection

5 Bassett-Lowke's rare gauge 0 LMS Pacific 'Coronation', which was available in either clockwork or electric, *circa* 1937.

4 Collectors attach considerable importance to this gauge 0 electric Märklin 'Cock O' the North' locomotive, *circa 1936*. It was rather an odd choice of contemporary prototype in view of the many other express locomotives which enjoyed popularity in British eyes at that time. However, the choice may have been influenced by the fact that this was one of the few English expresses to which the eight-coupled mechanism produced for the 'Mountain Etat' could be fitted.

1 A Märklin-bodied, Great Western, gauge 0 'King', fitted with the Bassett-Lowke permag electric mechanism, *circa 1935*, heads an Exley 'Ocean Mails' coach (probably post-war). Just visible, right, is a most unusual Exley Great Western 'Bullion' van, *circa 1937*.
(For Bassett-Lowke)

2 Front-end detail of a gauge 0 Märklin 'Cock O' the North'. (See fig. 4, page 117.)

3 A 'TCE 70' Tank locomotive for gauge 0 electric, with a 40 cm postal car for gauge 0. Both items by Märklin, *circa 1935*.

4 A gauge 0, Märklin-bodied Stanier 2–6–4 Tank, *circa 1936*, fitted with a Bassett-Lowke clockwork mechanism, illustrated with a Milbro 1st/3rd LMS Corridor coach.

5 A Northampton-produced, Bassett-Lowke, Great Western 'Prairie Tank' in gauge 0 electric, *circa 1937*, with a post-war 'Ocean Mails' by Exley for gauge 0. The post-war versions of Bassett-Lowke's 'Prairie Tanks' were made by V. Hunt exclusively for Bassett-Lowke, and were of totally different construction from their pre-war counterparts.

6 Leeds 0–4–4 electric Tank for 0 gauge, tentatively described as an ex-LSWR 'Adams T1' Tank, *circa 1935*. Also illustrated is a post-war Exley Southern 3rd Brake coach.

1 Leeds Model Company were the 'Jekyll and Hydes' of the trade. Models produced included several really dreadful freelance designs, a superb, super-detailed 'Flying Scotsman', and, as illustrated in this 1935 catalogue extract, a really excellent range of British Tank locomotives, all for electric running in gauge 0. Regrettably, Leeds' later diecast framed mechanisms did not live up to the excellence of their bodies. However, the Japanese firm of Stronlite saw fit to copy several Leeds designs during the 1930's. Below is a Leeds 1939 advertisement offering their unique Bakelite LMS coaches. They were the only European manufacturer to experiment with this material at this time.

VESTIBULE BRAKE COMPOSITE

ADD

DIGNITY

TO YOUR LAYOUT BY INCORPORATING

MOULDED ROLLING STOCK

BY THE

LEEDS MODEL CO., LTD.

POTTERDALE MILLS   LEEDS II

Descriptive leaflet free

Full Catalogue and leaflets **6d.**

Scale Model Tank Locomotives

THIS range of three scale tanks will, we feel sure, more than please all L.N.E.R. enthusiasts. The detail, high-class workmanship and general finish cannot be equalled, and the prototypes can be seen working on almost every part of the L.N.E.R. system.

SPECIFICATION.

BODY.   Best quality materials ; all joints soldered, not clipped ; diameter of boiler 1¼ ins.

POWER UNIT.   A.C. or D.C. mechanism (for descriptions see pages 44–46).

DETAILS.   Steps, handrails, brake pipes, smoke box door, and tank fillers are fitted.

0-4-4
G.C. 8120 Class
Cat. No.:
A.C. LA 10.
D.C. LD 10.

2-4-2
G.E. Class F.4.
Cat. No.
A.C. LA 11.
D.C. LD 11.

0-6-2
G.C. No. 5773.
Cat. No.
A.C. LA 12.
D.C. LD 12.

Price :

	A.C.		D.C.		
	LA 10	..	LD 10	..	£2 15 0
	LA 11	..	LD 11	..	£2 17 6
	LA 12	..	LD 12	..	£3 0 0

All fitted with double collectors.   Postage and packing free.

N.B. Before ordering see page 43, and then clearly state whether A.C. or D.C. unit is required, and give correct Catalogue No.

Scale Model Tank Locomotives

THESE three scale locomotives cater for the L.M.S. and S.R. enthusiasts. The wheel arrangements are particularly favoured in actual practice, and provide a choice of operating local passenger trains and fast goods traffic.

SPECIFICATION.

BODY.   Best quality materials ; all joints soldered, not clipped. Diameter of boiler, 1¼ ins.

POWER UNIT.   A.C. or D.C. mechanism (for description see pages 44–46).

DETAILS.   Steps, handrails, brake pipes, smoke box door, and tank fillers are fitted.

0-6-2 L.M.S.
(L. & Y.).
Cat. No. :
A.C. LA 20.
D.C. LD 20.

2-4-2 L.M.S.
(L. & Y.).
Horwich Rebuild.
Cat. No. :
A.C. LA 21.
D.C. LD 21.

0-4-4 S.R.
(L.S.W.R.).
Adams Class
T.1.
Ex. No. 3.
Cat. No. :
A.C. LA 22.
D.C. LD 22.

Price :

	A.C.		D.C.		
	LA 20	..	LD 20	..	£3 0 0
	LA 21	..	LD 21	..	£2 17 6
	LA 22	..	LD 22	..	£2 15 0

All fitted with double collectors.   Postage and packing free.

N.B. Before ordering see page 43, and then clearly state whether A.C. or D.C. unit is required, and give correct Catalogue No.

2 Hornby produced some very unremarkable tin lithographed trains in the United States. Illustrated here is a gauge 0, clockwork, locomotive and tender, *circa 1928*. *Photograph and Collection, Eduardo Lozano.*

3

The little Meccano engine from which has grown a huge industry—Hornby Trains.

3 Much discussion surrounds the definition of what was the first Hornby train, and although earlier reference has been made to Raylo, the following text which accompanied the little engine, reproduced from a Hornby pamphlet, and illustrated above, is self-explanatory: 'To really begin at the beginning we should have to take you back to the time of the 1914–1918 War. There were only a few toys available in those terrible days. Although there were at that time a few Meccano Outfits – but not nearly enough to go round – there were no toy trains at all, because before 1914 that kind of toy had always come from the Continent, and when hostilities broke out supplies were stopped. From all sides came the suggestion that Meccano Limited should produce clockwork trains, but at that time this was quite out of the question as almost our entire plant was engaged on war work. We did design a Meccano model of a locomotive, however, and we are giving you a peep of it. We treasure this little model more than you can imagine and we wouldn't sell it to anybody!'

1

2

1 A bird's-eye view of a goods depot provides an opportunity of showing a fine selection of Hornby's colourful gauge 0 wagons. The petrol tank wagons are some of the twenty or so different varieties available from 1921 to 1941. Many of the petrol brand names shown have long since disappeared, but they provide nostalgic memories of pre-war motoring days, as well as toy train operation! The engine in the foreground is a 1925 vintage 'No. 1' clockwork Tank. It is awaiting the loading of the final item of its mixed goods load before setting off.

R. Carss Collection

2 Royston Carss original drawing for the photographic set of the above picture.

3

3 'When Melancholy Autumn comes to Wembley, and electric trains are lighted after tea . . . .' So speaks Sir John Betjeman of Metroland, the region served by the Metropolitan line running from London through suburbia and westward to the Chiltern Hills. Here is Wembley re-created in tinplate by Hornby, with the 'Wembley' station and 'Metropolitan' train, both of which were introduced in 1925, at the time of the British Empire Exhibition at Wembley. The locomotive, produced in gauge 0, was originally sold in a 100/250 volt version (which proved highly dangerous), followed by 4 volt and clockwork, then 6 volt and finally 20 volt versions. Notice the bowler-hatted 'city gent' on the up-platform, peering anxiously for a glimpse of his train. Perhaps he is late for the office?   R. Carss Collection

4   Drawing for the above by Royston Carss.

1 An interesting LMS scene which provides a chance to compare two examples of the Hornby 'Big Engine' philosophy. On the left, the mighty 'Princess Elizabeth' Pacific, Hornby's largest ever engine, which was an immediate success when it was introduced in 1937. In contrast, the 'Royal Scot' on the right was, at very best, an approximation of the prototype, which was a 4–6–0 type, whereas the Hornby offering was a mere 4–4–2. (Both items gauge 0, for electric operation.) This deficiency did not appear to affect its sales, and it was produced from 1925 until 1941. The interesting array of accessories include an electrically lit 'No. 2' signal gantry and some 'Dinky Toys', which were introduced in 1933 by The Meccano Company to complement Hornby trains.

R. Carss Collection

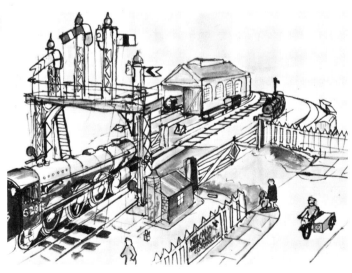

2 Royston Carss drawing for the above.

3

4

3 A splendid array of platform and lineside accessories clearly shows the immense possibilities of the Hornby system. The bustle of the busy station is well captured as the 'County of Bedford', *circa 1934,* in gauge 0 electric, arrives with a corridor-train consisting of main line coaches. The rear portion of the milk train stands in the siding, coupled to a four-wheeled GWR clerestory coach of 1928 vintage. The 'County of Bedford' was the GWR representative of the four 'No. 2 Special' series locomotives. (All four 'No. 2 Special' locomotives as introduced in 1929 were for clockwork only.)

R. Carss Collection

4 'Everyone loves the "Schools" Class engine', declared the 'Meccano Magazine' when their 'Eton' gauge 0 locomotive was introduced in 1937. Whether this was true is debatable, although the Hornby version was certainly popular. The engine was the first of the 'No. 4' series whose extension was regrettably curtailed by the outbreak of war. Hornby had by this time abandoned the use of the unsightly electric bulb on the smokebox door, as may be seen in this 20 volt version. The vehicle in the foreground is a tin-printed SR refrigeration van of the 'No. 0' series.

R. Carss Collection

1 The 'No. 2 Special' Hornby locomotive range was a commendable attempt to reproduce the 'true to type' features of certain locomotives. The 'Yorkshire' engine of the 'Shire' Class, shown here in electric, for gauge 0, was the LNER representative of this series, and was introduced in 1934. (Subsequently this model was up-dated to a 'Hunt' Class, and given the name 'Bramham Moor'.) The train of coaches complementing the engine is a rake of LNER tin-printed 'teak' stock, introduced in 1936 and available in the liveries of the four main-line companies. Although perhaps somewhat short in appearance they were a welcome change from the Saloons and Pullmans which had hitherto been the only main-line coaches available. R. Carss Collection

1

2

2 A gauge 0 'Compound', *circa 1934*, of the 'No. 2 Special' range brings its train around the curve, whilst the signalman looks on. The light-bulb in the electric versions of Hornby engines was considered by many to be an unsightly feature, although the factory undertook to supply the correct plain smokebox front, if specially requested. The trackwork is the special 'solid steel' 3ft radius type introduced specifically for the long wheelbase of the 'Princess Elizabeth' locomotives.

R. Carss Collection

3

3 Another 'No. 2 Special' or 'E220 Special', as the 20 volt electric versions were called. This time we are with the Southern Railway, and it is an 'L1' locomotive of 1934 in gauge 0, which is seen speeding away with the 'Dover Boat Train'. Possibly because of the geographical location of their factory (Liverpool), Hornby were loathe to acknowledge the existence of the Southern; indeed, *no* Southern items were produced in the early days of Hornby trains. R. Carss Collection

4

4 The French 'Blue Train', with its exciting and adventurous Agatha Christie associations, was introduced by Hornby as early as 1926, and a clockwork version is shown (centre) with its 'Dining' and 'Sleeping' cars. The locomotive was a variation of the body used on the 'Royal Scot' and some other types of express locomotives. The stream-lined SNCF train in the background is a 20 volt set produced by Meccano in their Paris factory in the early post-war years. The three items of French rolling stock in the front sidings were produced in Liverpool for the British and French markets. All items for gauge 0. R. Carss Collection

1 A busy scene at a Hornby railway running shed. Several locomotives are seen preparing for their day's work. Two brass-domed, gauge 0, clockwork Tank locomotives – a 4–4–4 and an 0–4–0, *circa 1925*, are about to receive attention with the oil can, whilst two 'No. 1 Special' Tank locomotives, *circa 1929*, and a 'County' are awaiting refreshment from the water tank in the background. Hornby were very conscious of promoting 'real' railway practice, and frequent articles in the monthly 'Meccano Magazine' kept boys in touch with the latest railway developments, and with the latest additions to the Hornby range.   R. Carss Collection

3 This unique model of the 'Beyer-Ljungstrom' Turbo-condensing locomotive (the prototype was used experimentally by the LMS) for gauge 0, was produced by the Leeds Model Company to special order. It features the extremely competent bodywork achieved by that firm, and this particular model was intended for layout running in electric, *circa 1928*. (This model was in fact built by J. S. Beeson to the order of the Leeds Model Company.)

4 A Northampton built, gauge 0 'A4' Pacific in electric, *circa 1936*, heads a 'Silver Jubilee' train on the special layout constructed by Bassett-Lowke for the Glasgow Exhibition of 1938. Bassett-Lowke stream-lined locomotives, particularly the 'A4's, are extraordinarily rare, and it is doubtful whether more than 200 of all three versions of the LNER engine were ever built.

2 The LMS were the only British railway company to experiment operationally with a steam turbine, and Bassett-Lowke produced a small batch of these model locomotives in gauge 0 electric, *circa 1937*, which were in fact constructed from components used in the 'Princess Royal' type Pacific models introduced in 1933. (See fig. 6.)
Count Giansanti Collection

5 Bassett-Lowke live steam 'Super Enterprise' in LNER livery, for gauge 0, heads a train comprising Milbro all wooden-bodied coaches. *Circa 1936*.

6 It is exciting to remember how quickly model makers could turn out the latest prototypes such was the public interest in any new prototype steam locomotives during this period; as illustrated here by an advertisement from the December 1933 edition of 'Practical Mechanics'. (The model depicted was one of a small series, built by J. S. Beeson, on a sub-contract basis for Bassett-Lowke, which was followed by the more numerous Winteringham version.)

The photograph shows a fine Bassett Lowke O gauge model of the new L.M.S. locomotive, The Princess Royal, which was recently completed at Crewe and designed by the new locomotive superintendent. This model is electrically propelled by an 8-pole motor.

1 A Bassett-Lowke Southern 'Mogul' in steam for gauge 0, *circa 1926*, heads a train of 1931-series Bassett-Lowke coaches. The Southern and Great Western versions of the 'Mogul', sold disappointingly, and relatively few were produced compared with the LMS and LNER liveried versions.

2 Reflecting Bassett-Lowke's somewhat bland approach in its style of manufacture is this three-car gauge 0 Central Line Underground set in electric, originally made for the London Passenger Board's Exhibition Layout at Charing Cross in 1934. Later the item was catalogued and manufactured as a standard line. The cars were fabricated in sheet brass, and relatively few sets were produced. (A very superior gauge 0 lithographed tinplate electric train known as the 'Euston/Watford Set' was produced by Winteringham for Bassett-Lowke in 1930, and was virtually the first lithographed model to incorporate the lessons of Bing in a British-produced tinplate item.)

3 One of Bassett-Lowke's cheapest prototype models was the extremely attractive gauge 0 LMS 'Compound' available in clockwork or electric. For some reason many of these models appeared in a very attractive – if unusual – chestnut livery. The example illustrated is an electric version, *circa 1928* hauling a train which includes a 1931 series LMS coach (British-made) and a twelve-wheeled LMS 'Dining Saloon', a development of Carette's original LNWR version.

4

5

4 A pair of electric Märklin 00 scale trains of the immediate pre-war period. At left, a 4–6–4 'SK 800' modelled on the class 'BR 06' (prototype 4–8–4) of the Deutsche Reichsbahngesellschaft by Krupp of which only two prototype engines were built. At right, a much modelled 'Pacific' at the head of a 25cm D. Zugwagen. At this stage, Märklin's range of H0 material was way ahead of its competitors.

5 Various Bing 00 sets (here advertised in the 1924 Gamage catalogue) marked the beginning of this gauge as a serious concept. Boxed sets as comprehensive as this were not to be repeated in later years.

6 It is interesting to compare this post-war revival by Märklin of its H0 'SK 800' locomotive, first introduced in 1939, with its predecessor in fig. 4. Märklin are one of the few European manufacturers to have continued with the extensive use of metal diecast bodies for their locomotives. Hornby, of course, persisted with this material until their absorption by Triang, at which time Wrenn acquired the tooling and still continue to market metal diecast 00 locomotives under their own label. *Official photograph by courtesy of Märklin, retouched for catalogue use.*

6

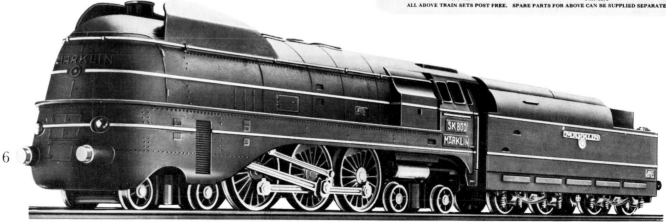

1 Lionel's only contribution in 00 for 19mm gauge was this excellent 'Hudson' in electric, which was only issued as a freight set in 1938. These trains were not, in fact, revived after the second world war. The appendage on the tank car is a later addition.

2 A massive 00 4–6–4 by Scale-Craft, utilising heavy brass castings, for 19mm gauge, two-rail running, *circa 1937*. The products of this firm, together with those of Varney and Mantua, signify the real beginnings of scale modelling in the U.S. in the smaller gauges. In some ways the construction of this locomotive is reminiscent of early American cast iron models. This example of an American 00 locomotive weighed over 4lbs.

5 Illustrated here is the culmination of Lionel's gauge 0 diecast production, as advertised in the British edition of their 1939 catalogue.

3

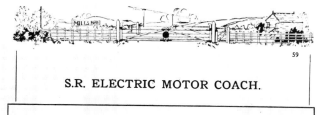

59

S.R. ELECTRIC MOTOR COACH.

The body work is made on our well-known principle, having glazed windows. The motor-man's driving end is fitted with glass windows and louvre ventilators. The finish is as our standard coaches. Fitted with a powerful 6—8 volt permanent magnet motor, tripolar armature.

G 0 only ... ... **£4 7s. 6d.** each.
Trailer Coaches for attaching to the above. See our S.R. Standard Coaches for prices.

METROPOLITAN MOTOR COACH.

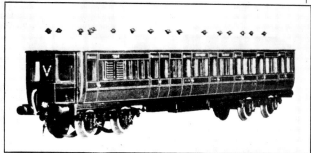

Specification as foregoing S.R. Electric Motor Coach, G 0 only, **£3 15s.**
Trailer Coaches for attaching to the above, **35/-** each.

3 Mills Brothers, trading as 'Milbro', were noted principally for their excellent, wood-fabricated, passenger stock. The examples in this extract from their catalogue indicate how inappropriate wood was as a medium for modelling the rebuilt 'Metropolitan' locomotive, *circa 1930*. Nonetheless, they marketed a limited range of metal locomotives including a gauge 0 version of the 'Cock O' the North'.

4 With the demise of Bing, Bassett-Lowke sought to concentrate upon tin-lithographed production in Britain, and in 1931, they introduced a series of coaches (which were 14″ long as opposed to 13″ for the Bing series), to supersede the earlier 1921 series. Here we have an example of a GWR 3rd Composite coach in gauge 0. It is interesting to compare this 1931-series coach with the GWR clerestory coaches, produced some twenty years earlier, by Carette in gauge 0, forming the rake illustrated above. *(For Bassett-Lowke)*

1931-series GWR coach – Torry Collection

1 Walkers & Holtzapffel supplied several narrow gauge locomotives in electric, for operation on gauge 0 track. This particular example of a Peckett Tank 'Kitchener' was one of the super-detailed models made to order by that firm in the 1930's. (In fact, several of these Tanks were made for Walkers & Holtzapffel by J. S. Beeson.) Walkers & Holtzapffel continued their business as wholesalers to the model trade, and in later years, the firm's name has been abbreviated to W & H Models.

2 And now for something completely different! – A bizarre locomotive made up from a one-hundred-part construction set manufactured by Primus Engineering. This clockwork locomotive, *circa 1924*, is nominally gauge 1. It is understood that there were legal problems with Meccano Limited, in view of the similarity of certain components with those produced by the latter firm.

4 The boy pictured on the box is evidently extolling the virtues of the Hornby 'Dublo' train-set contained therein. In this case, it is the stream-lined 'Sir Nigel Gresley' engine, with its pair of articulated coaches, introduced in 1938. This was Hornby's first venture into 00 or 'Dublo' as they termed it. This example is clockwork, but the set was also available in a 12 volt electric version, as was the Tank goods set also illustrated. 'Dublo' was obviously expected to be 'the gauge of the future', but the outbreak of hostilities temporarily curtailed its development. After the war it gained in popularity to the extent of ousting 0 gauge from the Hornby range almost entirely.

R. Carss Collection

3 This picture illustrates the overlap that took place in the early 1930's when certain Continental manufacturers were the subject of partial and total 'takeovers'. A 00 clockwork, Bub train, *circa 1930*, is flanked by two Bub stations, while in the background, a Bing-produced Great Western 00 clockwork Tank, *circa 1923*, stands outside a Bing-made locomotive shed. The car partly shown is a rare U.S. variant of Bing's 00 series.

1

1 A pause to see where we have come so far: a Märklin gauge 1, clockwork 0–2–2 dating from the end of the nineteenth century alongside a gauge 1 Märklin 'Pacific' in electric, which marked the end of this era.   M. Darphin Collection

2

2 First cataloguing of the Hornby 'Dublo' electric 'Duchess of Atholl' with single chimney, in 'The Hornby Book of Trains' for 1939. While these models were officially introduced in 1939, they were apparently not available until after the second world war.

3 Cut-out models of all types have been popular during the ages, particularly in the austerity period after the second world war. One of the largest ranges of cut-out railway models was issued by Micromodels Limited of London in the 1950's, and a typical cross-section of these products is illustrated.

THE POST WAR ERA

The decline of gauge 0, unquestionably the most popular pre-war system, accelerated in the post-war years, and volume manufacturers who failed to face the reality of that trend had disappeared by the early 1960's.

Meccano Limited continued to develop its pre-war Hornby Dublo range, but it basked too long in its earlier success and eventually failed in 1964 when, ironically enough, all but its model railway products were entering boom conditions.

Triang, through its Rovex subsidiary, introduced a perfectly practicable two-rail 00 system in 1952, but the model railway products of that company never really matched the vastly improved standards demanded both on the Continent and in America. Triang also launched a TT-3 range (scale 1:102) in 1959, which proved to be an evolutionary dead end (as was the 13mm gauge produced by Wesa in Switzerland), although Zeuke of East Germany continued to market TT (scale 1:120) as did Rokal in West Germany for a time. Towards the end of 1971 Triang, which had previously absorbed Meccano Limited, ceased trading as an entity, and Hornby trains passed on yet again, in the absorption of Triang by Dunbee-Combex.

The final demise of Winteringham (by this time re-named Precision Model Railways Limited and almost totally committed to the manufacture of Trix products) was brought about by the failure of Trix of Great Britain in the late 1950's. Trix of Great Britain continued to operate under a variety of patronages during the 1960's and subsequently launched an excellent range of British outline locomotives for 00. It finally ceased production in Britain during 1973, although Trix of Germany – after several further changes in ownership – still continued and at the present time forms part of a toy-making group known as Trix Mangold.

Against all the trends in Europe, Märklin persisted with its H0 centre pick-up stud AC system, while firms such as Fleischmann, Liliput and Rivarossi, became the supreme exponents of high-quality, two-rail DC, H0 scale model trains. Jouef of France (marketed as 'Playcraft' in Great Britain) and Lima of Italy supplied the medium priced H0 model train market.

4 From left to right: (in the background) Tom Snoxell, the Author, and Harry Amey at the Model Engineer Exhibition at Seymour Hall, 1968, during the launching of the new Bassett-Lowke (Railways) Limited line. The locomotives featured are, at left, the original 'Stirling Single' in live steam for gauge 1 by Gianini and Mühlethaler (more on which later), and at right, the prototype of a gauge 1, 'Wainwright D', in electric, built by French, Hefford and Littledale. A little later the tender to the 'Wainwright' locomotive was stolen. Perhaps this event was portentious as the locomotive never went into production as planned.

In the post-war period, plastic model kits became a vast new industry, but apart from buildings and lineside accessories, they encompassed relatively few railway subjects. In Britain, the majority of locomotive kits comprised white metal castings put out by such firms as Wills, Keyser and Jamieson, whereas in America, a bewildering array of locomotive and coach kits were available, ranging from sophisticated brass castings for locomotives to mixtures of wood and metal for passenger and freight cars. Kits for locomotives and rolling stock did not achieve any great popularity in Europe, although Rivarossi marketed some of its locomotives in 'knocked down' form.

1

2

1 Lithographed tinplate, friction-driven, floor train by Daiya of Japan, *circa 1960*. A string pulled at one end of this toy produces the most alarming horn sound. This is an excellent illustration of the manner in which the Japanese toy industry continued the use of photolithography on tinplate, in the post war era. (Track width $1\frac{1}{2}''$.)

2 This picture illustrates the appealing brashness of Japanese lithographed floor toys of the 1960's. The friction toy on the left, named the 'Euro Express', screams along the floor, whirring and whistling (bears trade mark ATC). Alongside, is a somewhat more accurate interpretation of a Japanese National Railway CoCo. This battery operated locomotive is fitted with a patent device (used on so many Japanese toys) which enables it to turn on its own axis when it comes into contact with an obstacle (bears trade mark BCE). (Track widths: $1\frac{7}{8}''$ and $2\frac{3}{4}''$ respectively.)

In the United States, ready-to-run trains under the Lionel label were still produced for 0 gauge and for a short time their production was concentrated in Japan. The ownership of the Lionel Corporation was to pass through various hands, and at one time it was under the unlikely control of a Mr. Roy M. Cohn, more widely known for his associations with Senator McCarthy and a very 'special' brand of railroading! During the 1950's S gauge, which was never popular outside the United States, was marketed principally by Gilbert, still using the American Flyer label. By the early 1970's virtually all the major US model train producers were subsidiaries of various giant food

corporations. I am not certain what the moral of this is, but one statistic that may be relevant is that the model railway hobby in the US at the present time accounts for retail sales in excess of forty-million dollars per annum.

A most significant development in model railways came about as a direct result of the very close post-war trading links established by Japan and the United States. This led to the manufacture of high quality, brass, batch-produced scale locomotives (principally for 0 and H0). The Japanese model railway industry was supported by an infra-structure of small back-street manufacturers, some of whom

may have been responsible for manufacturing a single component, such as a Westinghouse Pump, utilising, in the main, the 'lost wax' casting process.

Component parts were then assembled by the larger corporations such as Tenshodo and KTM before being exported to the USA for distribution, largely by firms which had sponsored the particular batch of models as principals. One of the few European importers to engage in this method of production was Fulgurex – and somewhat later Metropolitan – (both of Switzerland) and collectors may be grateful to those firms for the European prototypes which were manufactured in this way. The only Japanese-produced, brass, British-outline locomotive, was an LMS 'Crab' for H0, although a GWR 'King' class locomotive for H0 was initiated by Fulgurex, only to be abandoned several years later owing to errors in the scale of the production prototype.

After several false alarms, the mid-sixties saw the real rise of N gauge (9 mm) as a serious alternative to H0/00 scales, and most major Continental manufacturers produced N gauge variants of their popular H0 ranges for both the European and the American market. Once again British manufacturers seemed to miss this phase (despite the British firm of 'Lone Star' having been pioneers in this field), but Peco of Seaton had the foresight to sponsor the production – through Rivarossi – of an excellent 'Jubilee' locomotive of N gauge.

Whereas specialised firms continued their production of quality gauge 0 items, few were ready for the impact which would be made at the 1969 Nuremburg Toy Fair, when major manufacturers such as Rivarossi and Pola Maxi plunged into the market at the deep end with a range of high volume, injection moulded, scale plastic trains for gauge 0. Perhaps this development was spurred on by the relative success of Lehmann's 'Grossbahn', introduced in 1968, although this was in effect a narrow gauge system – equivalent to the earlier scale for gauge 3, but for gauge 1 track. At about this time, Triang introduced its 0 gauge 'Big, Big Train' series as did Lego and somewhat later, Faller, these systems being unquestionably aimed at the true 'juvenile play-market'. However, no such categoric claims can be made for the other makers discussed here. Experience since that time suggests that the high-volume market for 0 gauge scale trains is likely to prove illusory, and it would not be surprising if the production of 0 gauge equipment once again reverted to a few specialised firms and builders.

Märklin, who were prominent towards the beginning of our story, joined the 'big gauge fray' in 1969 with a gauge 1 system, and a little later introduced a narrow gauge system in 7mm scale for H0 track known as 'Minex', and a sub N gauge system – Z gauge – marketed as 'Mini-Club'.

It is fitting that our chronological review should end with a panorama of Märklin products (see page 176) which illustrates the story of reduction in scale without any real concessions to detail or fidelity.

3

Looking back on the progressive reduction of scale over the century, it would appear that the pendulum has come to rest at H0/00 scale railways (despite the real challenge of the micro-gauges) in much the same way as it rested with 0 gauge in the inter-war years. There may be even the further progression down the scale, though in collecting terms, it is difficult to imagine a generation hence scouring their lands for N or Z (or even Z^n) gauge plastic trains. Yet, it would have been equally as difficult to have predicted the collecting zeal of this and previous generations. I think what may become evident is that the time lag between product obsolescence and its elevation to an object worthy of collection may diminish to a point where, like Californian wine, vintage may no longer be an overriding consideration.

3 The Japanese contribution to post-war railway models was at opposite extremes of the industry. On the one hand they were to dominate the top end of the H0 scale and 0 gauge market with batch-produced brass locomotives, constructed with castings produced on the 'lost-wax' principle, while on the other they were to produce lithographed tin toys which were, in reality, a continuation of the tradition established by the earlier German toy makers. Illustrated, is a friction driven floor train, *circa 1955*, and it is unusual in that apart from being designated 'New York Central', it is a reasonably faithful model of a Japanese National Railway 2–6–4 and tender (bears the trade mark SAN). Normally, this type of toy would be produced with even less pretence of prototype appearance. (Track width $1\frac{1}{2}''$.)

1 This picture, which might be entitled 'Great Expectations', shows that the tradition of misleading but charming train set box-tops continued well into the post-war years. Chad Valley made tinplate toys until the 1960's, but their gauge 0 trains were, at best, a primitive imitation of Hornby's post-war range. (See 'Recent Locomotives 1947–70' by P. E. Randall.)

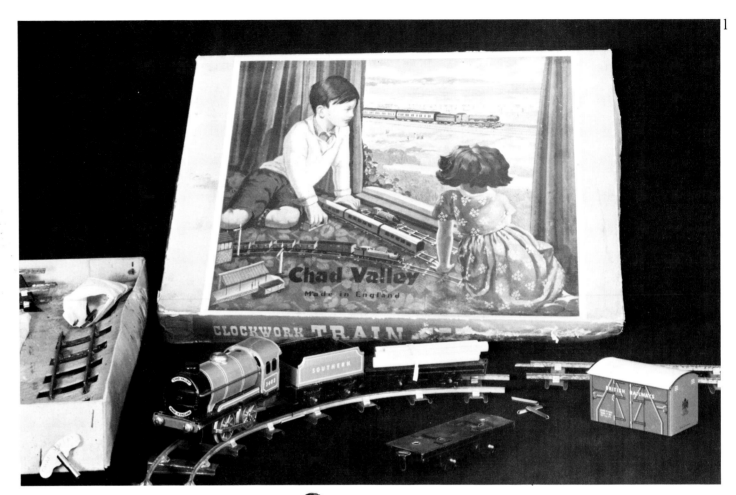

2 Most of the pre-war equipment illustrated in this magnificent Hornby layout was available for a short time when stocks were 'unfrozen' in 1947. Very few of the items were catalogued thereafter.

3 This London Underground set in battery-operated 00 scale, was the sole excursion into model train manufacturing of the Ever Ready Company, one of the largest battery manufacturers in the United Kingdom. The rolling stock was exceptionally crude by the standards of the day, and the range, like any model railway system that did not offer the opportunity of expansion, was soon to disappear. *Circa 1953.*

4 A line up of typical British, post-war austerity, clockwork, floor toys. The green 'Ubilda' Tank locomotive was by Burnett, later taken over by Chad Valley, who issued the red version as illustrated (track width 1¾"). Typical tinplate buses of this period by Wells.

5 Another remarkable illustration of the disparity between box-top advertising and actual content, is this Paya train set, *circa 1965.*

1 From 1940 onwards, Keiser of Zug in Switzerland turned out gauge 0 electric locomotives which appeared to be manufactured in the best traditions of Swiss instrument makers. Illustrated along the line are a pair of 'E 3/3' steam-outline locomotives, whilst on the outside line is a freight train, headed by an 'Ee 3/3', *circa 1955*. The 'Weiacher Kies' Hopper car is by an obscure Swiss manufacturer named Schardt, and the 'Interfrigo' car is by Darstaed. Both date from the late 1960's.

Torry Collection

2 HAG of Switzerland (H. & A. Gahler), produced more life-like trains between 1939 and the early 1950's, particularly, this very fine SBB CFF 'Re 4/4' in electric for gauge 0, *circa 1947*. The locomotive is depicted with an SBB car by Hermann of Switzerland, *circa 1970*. By the late 1950's, both HAG and BUCO, who appeared during the war-time absence of Märklin, had ceased 0 gauge production. (Although HAG continued with its H0 line.) The firm of Erno, a further Swiss manufacturer specialising in gauge 0, also disappeared shortly after the second world war.

BUCO - Personenzüge * Trains de voyageurs BUCO

No. P 212/12 (54,5 cm) Fr. 49.80
No. P 301/12 Fr. 77.—

No. P 212/13 (73 cm) Fr. 61.50
No. P 301/13 Fr. 87.—

No. P 212/13 = 1 No. 212 + 2 No. 8671 + 1 No. 8672 + 8 75 A M 75 AE · 4 75 D M 75 DE + 2 KK
No. P 301/13 = 1 No. 301

No. P 212/12 = 1 No. 212 + 2 No. 8671 + 8 75 A M 75 AE · 2 75 D M 75 DE + 2 KK
No. P 301/12 = 1 No. 301

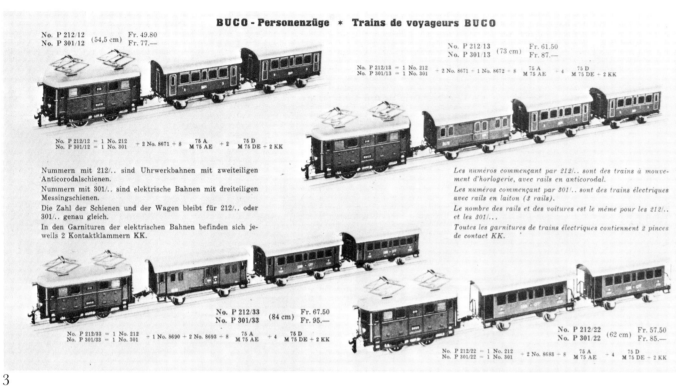

Nummern mit 212/.. sind Uhrwerkbahnen mit zweiteiligen Anticorodalschienen.
Nummern mit 301/.. sind elektrische Bahnen mit dreiteiligen Messingschienen.
Die Zahl der Schienen und der Wagen bleibt für 212/.. oder 301/.. genau gleich.
In den Garnituren der elektrischen Bahnen befinden sich jeweils 2 Kontaktklammern KK.

Les numéros commençant par 212/.. sont des trains à mouvement d'horlogerie, avec rails en anticorodal.
Les numéros commençant par 301/.. sont des trains électriques avec rails en laiton (3 rails).
Le nombre des rails et des voitures est le même pour les 212/.. et les 301/..
Toutes les garnitures de trains électriques contiennent 2 pinces de contact KK.

No. P 212/33 (84 cm) Fr. 67.50
No. P 301/33 Fr. 95.—

No. P 212/33 = 1 No. 212 + 1 No. 8690 + 2 No. 8693 + 8 75 A M 75 AE · 4 75 D M 75 DE + 2 KK
No. P 301/33 = 1 No. 301

No. P 212/22 (62 cm) Fr. 57.50
No. P 301/22 Fr. 85.—

No. P 212/22 = 1 No. 212 + 2 No. 8683 + 8 75 A M 75 AE · 4 75 D M 75 DE + 2 KK
No. P 301/22 = 1 No. 301

3

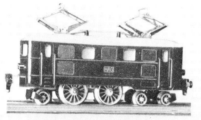

Dimensions Grösse
250 | 120 | 70

Dimensions Grösse
180 | 120 | 70

Dimensions Grösse
240 | 120 | 70

Loko 11852 F
Sfr. 90.-

Loko 1946 F
Sfr. 57.-

Loko 1101 F
Sfr. 90.-

avec commande à distance. Couleur verte
courant de traction 8-18 V; courant de retour 27 V
trois lampes AV, une lampe AR
raccordement de lumière pour l'éclairage des wagons

avec commande à distance. Couleur verte
courant de traction 8-18 V; courant de retour 27 V
2 lampes AV

avec commande à distance. Couleur verte ou brune
courant de traction 8-18 V; courant de retour 27 V
trois lampes AV, une lampe AR
raccordement de lumière pour l'éclairage des wagons

mit Fernsteuerung. Farbe grün
Fahrstrom 8-18 V; Umschaltstrom 27 V
3 Stirnlampen, 1 rotes Schlusslicht
Anschluss für Wagenbeleuchtung

mit Fernsteuerung. Farbe grün
Fahrstrom 8-18 V; Umschaltstrom 27 V
2 Stirnlampen

mit Fernsteuerung. Farbe grün oder braun
Fahrstrom 8-18 V; Umschaltstrom 27 V
3 Stirnlampen, 1 rotes Schlusslicht
Anschluss für Wagenbeleuchtung

HAG

4

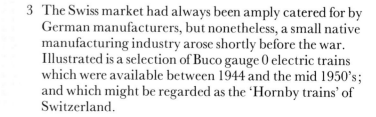

4 Some of the last tinplate clockwork trains available in Europe were from Biller of West Germany for 16.5mm gauge. Included in this illustration of Biller items is an engine shed which is unique, in that it enabled a locomotive to be wound up while standing in it, and started by putting a finger through the hole in the shed roof and pressing the start button. Perhaps these labour-saving devices were a sign of the post-war years, and in fact, these little trains, including a steam outline Tank locomotive in plastic, were available until the early 1970's. In 1974 the line was re-introduced utilising many more plastic components.

3 The Swiss market had always been amply catered for by German manufacturers, but nonetheless, a small native manufacturing industry arose shortly before the war. Illustrated is a selection of Buco gauge 0 electric trains which were available between 1944 and the mid 1950's; and which might be regarded as the 'Hornby trains' of Switzerland.

1

2

New York, Philadelphia, Chicago and all points West!

Who-o-o
Who-o-o

American Flyer through train!

Hiss-s-s-s

All Aboard!

Chug-Chug

1 Louis Marx and Co. of the USA were not noted for their contribution to the model railway scene, but this little post-war 2–4–2 electric locomotive for gauge 0, in Canadian Pacific livery, *circa 1954*, together with its train of Pullmans named after the Provinces, was a brave enough attempt.

799 $19.95

No. 799 AUTOMATIC TALKING STATION

American Flyer's famous Talking Station, newly-designed to make it better than ever! When you press remote control button, this is what happens automatically: your train stops in front of the station, and while it waits you hear sounds right from the station interior — hissing steam, piston chugs, trainmaster's voice, etc. When sounds cease, train automatically resumes trip. Entire operation is electrical — no batteries required. Don't confuse this station with others which do far, far less. Dimensions: 16″ long, 8¾″ high, 9″ wide.

2 American lineside accessories really came into their own with Ives lineside accessories, followed by Lionel's famous tinplate stations, power houses and bridges of the 1930's. In the post war era, apart from the very wide selection of plastic lineside construction kits available from Continental manufacturers such as Vollmer, Faller and Kibri, many specialist American firms produced lineside feature kits to very high specifications, particularly for the H0 market. The water tower (fig. 5) was produced as a kit by Lehigh Valley Models for the S gauge market. By way of contrast, is an illustration of one of Gilbert American Flyer's last S gauge stations, which speaks for itself! *Circa 1954.*
Photo of Water Tower by courtesy of Floyd E. McEachern

5

3 Paya of Spain, had a particularly basic approach to modelling. The train illustrated is the top of the range, gauge 0 electric set, but the locomotive left much to be desired in its mechanical performance. Nevertheless, it was one of the last tinplate electric, gauge 0 systems available, *circa 1960*.

3

4

4 This diminutive 4–4–0 American 'Wood Burner' is purported to be a handmade, factory produced prototype for a post-war gauge 0 electric product, by Gebr. Fleischmann, *circa 1950*. In the event, Fleischmann wisely decided to concentrate on their H0 range, and this little prototype presumably found its way out of that firm's development department. The train is made-up with two open-end cars, in wood, constructed from OGA kits.

6

6 A Bassett-Lowke, live-steam, gauge 0 'Super Enterprise' on a garden layout, *circa 1940*.

1

2

1 A trio of late 1960 offerings in plastic:– An 'Indiana Harbor Belt' locomotive for gauge 0, electric, an H0 version (centre) in special gold finish and, partly shown, a Southern 'Pacific' for N gauge. The first two are by Rivarossi, the third by Arnold.

2 AHM NYC Japanese brass 4–4–0 and tender in electric for H0, *circa 1963*, with a 'Barnum' special advertising coach and the 'Lincoln Funeral' car, both former Pocher items by Rivarossi, *circa 1965*.

3

3 Normally Japanese locomotives were delivered in their natural brass, leaving it to local importers to determine the finish. Here we have an example of the legendary Union Pacific 'Big Boy' for 0 gauge, with its twin articulated, electric driving assemblies. This model was the epitome of the standards achieved from the early 1950's onwards, when this type of production commenced, and it is doubtful whether it could be materially bettered by a one-off model. The 'Big Boy' locomotives were produced in batches of 100 to 150, and this particular example is one of a batch made by KTM, *circa 1967*. At the time of writing, a further batch of these models is being produced for various importers, but it has become increasingly difficult for Japanese producers to maintain the high standards reached in the mid-sixties. It would appear that what was basically a 'cottage-craft' industry, has succumbed to the demands of Japan's burgeoning factories. Giving the picture scale is a typical kit-produced locomotive (from Japanese brass parts), thought to have been supplied by Westside for H0n3 scale, together with cars produced from wooden components.

4

4 This gauge 0, electric powered, Pennsylvania M.1.a. 4–8–2 'Mountain' type by KTM is representative of Japanese brass construction at its zenith during the early 1960's. This particular model was imported into America through the agency of Max Gray in 1961. As previously mentioned, Japanese manufacturers were commissioned to build comparatively few European types, but then the American post-war market achieved a degree of sophistication, refinement and spending power which completely reversed the pre-war roles of the two great model railway centres.

1

1 An all brass Southern Pacific 'General Motors' Diesel in
H0 by Tenshodo, *circa 1965*, alongside a superb diecast
'Sante Fe' Diesel by Märklin, for H0 electric, *circa 1962*.
Note : Märklin and Fleischmann in particular, produced
metal diecast mouldings to an exceptionally high
standard, although during 1967 the latter firm went over
to the almost exclusive use of plastic, taking that
opportunity to reduce the scale of its H0 trains from 1 :82
to 1 :87 scale.

2

3

3 A Gilbert/American Flyer, Union Pacific 'Northern' 4–8–4 for S (half gauge 1) gauge in electric, *circa 1954*. Additional features included with this model are red glowing smoke and air chime whistle with remote control.

2 At the same time as Märklin were offering the last of their 0 gauge clockwork range, they introduced this unusual 0–4–0 in clockwork for H0, *circa 1953*. The style of this plastic-bodied 'beginners' engine is presumably a dwarfed version of the giant 'Pennsylvania' stream-line types.

4 Meanwhile, 'back at the Ranch', Lionel was producing many excellent Diesel locomotives, and some less admirable steam-outline prototypes. Apart from its standard range of locomotives and rolling stock, Lionel produced many special train sets, as indicated in the catalogue extract illustrated, *circa 1964*. The products of Lionel prove that items produced in plastic are not necessarily barred from becoming 'collectables', as demonstrated by the old-time set featured in the illustration. The tradition of collecting 'instant obsolesence' is firmly established in America, and despite the obvious pitfalls, it is rapidly gaining ground in Europe. *By courtesy of The Lionel Corp.*

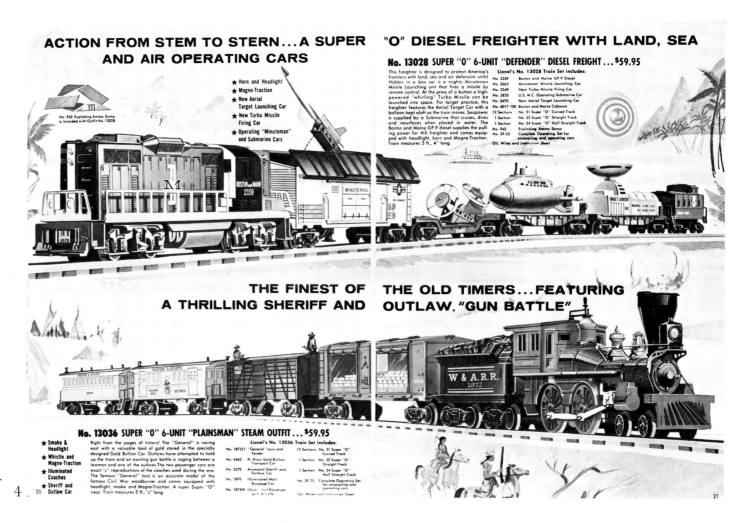

ACTION FROM STEM TO STERN...A SUPER AND AIR OPERATING CARS

"O" DIESEL FREIGHTER WITH LAND, SEA

THE FINEST OF A THRILLING SHERIFF AND

THE OLD TIMERS...FEATURING OUTLAW, "GUN BATTLE"

1 A fine example of the work of H. Clarkson of York is this very atmospheric model of Thompson's B1 Class locomotive, 'Sir Geoffrey Gibb'. The locomotive was built in 1950 for electric running in gauge 1. This model illustrates how a reduction of 1 : 32, (10mm/1ft) is possibly the smallest scale by which the optical illusion of the essential coarseness of a prototype locomotive can be conveyed.

2 2½″ gauge is generally accepted as the largest practical gauge for scenic running. This gauge was particularly popular in Great Britain, and the two live steam, coal fired locomotives illustrated, are amongst the finest examples of commercial work in this scale. Both have the capacity to haul passengers. The 'Coronation' Class Pacific was completed in 1939 by H. P. Jackson of York, who later made a set of castings available for this model. The stream-lined casing was constructed from 20-gauge brass, and hand-beaten to shape. This remarkable model includes a set of four working cylinders, as in the prototype. The 'A3', at right, was built in 1953 by H. Clarkson & Son, who also, incidentally, acquired the drawings and parts which survived a disastrous fire in H. P. Jackson's workshop shortly before his death. The 'A3' had steam brakes, but was fitted with two cylinders and not three as in the prototype.   'A3' – Torry Collection

4

3

4 The final version of Bassett-Lowke's electric 'Compound' for 0 gauge, *circa 1950*, is seen with Bassett-Lowke's last series of coaches in the short-lived BR lake and cream livery (photographed during a platelayers' strike!). The train represents virtually the last quantity produced lithographed tinplate items by Bassett-Lowke, which were available until the early 1960's, and this locomotive and two coaches were, in fact, offered as a boxed set, a relatively late innovation for Bassett-Lowke. (See also fig. 3, page 130.)

3 One of Bassett-Lowke's superb series of 'Cock O' the North' locomotives, in live steam for 2½″ gauge. Probably one of the most beautiful batch-built locomotives ever produced.

1 Bassett-Lowke's finest, British-made, lithographed tinplate model was undoubtedly the 0 gauge 'Flying Scotsman', first produced at the Winteringham factory in Northampton in 1932, and offered in clockwork or electric. The model continued in production in the post-war period, and this illustration indicates one of the last LNER versions, in electric, *circa 1950*, bearing the pre-nationalisation number '103' in place of the more famous '4472', which that locomotive bore until 1946.

2 Gauge 0 'Flying Scotsman' in electric, in British Railways experimental blue livery, *circa 1950*.

3 A final version in standard BR green livery for electric operation, *circa 1955*.

4 One of the penultimate batch of gauge 0, live steam, Bassett-Lowke 'Moguls', *circa 1965*, heading a train of Winteringham's excellently produced pre-war tank wagons. (BR-liveried 'Moguls' were numbered 42980.) A final batch of live steam 'Moguls' were produced in association with Bassett-Lowke (Railways) Limited, and these were all in either LMS black or red, numbered in sequence from 13000. The re-introduction of this model at a relatively high price – 1926: 5 guineas, 1969: £105.00 including purchase tax – stimulated others to produce small batches of gauge 0 and 1 live steam locomotives on a commercial basis. Archangel Models, who commenced business at about this time, appear to have established a niche for themselves in small scale live steam, specialising in narrow gauge types, mainly in 16mm scale, for running on 0 gauge track.

5 An austere post-war version of Bassett-Lowke's 0–6–0 and tender in electric, for gauge 0, *circa 1950*. The Guards' vans illustrated also typify the peculiarly dull appearance of so many Northampton-built items of the immediate post-war era.

1 A rare model of the rebuilt 'Royal Scot'. This locomotive was one of the last series of tinplate locomotives built by Bassett-Lowke in gauge 0, for electric running, *circa 1956*.

2 Bassett-Lowke produced one diesel prototype for their regular 0 gauge electric range, and once again the bodywork for this series was specifically made by V. Hunt for that company. These models were available in BR green and English Electric blue liveries. On the left is the original Bassett-Lowke 'Deltic', *circa 1963*, finished in BR green livery. The 'Deltic' standing alongside in the alternative blue livery, *circa 1972*, gives an indication of how the second series might have looked had V. Reader remained associated with the revival of the Bassett-Lowke *marque* in 1968. In the event, only a small batch of the Reader locomotives were produced. The picture also illustrates how scale conception in the medium quality market had changed, even within a decade.

3

3 Billy Gordon, who gave over 50 years service at Bassett-Lowke in Northampton, working on part of the last batch of live steam, gauge 0, Stanier 'Moguls', produced exclusively for the new Bassett-Lowke (Railways) Limited company during 1969.

5 During the heady days of 1968 plans were well advanced for producing an entirely new, popularly priced, live steam locomotive, for gauge 0, by Bassett-Lowke (Railways) Limited, in collaboration with the original company in Northampton. The little factory-produced prototype Tank locomotive was loosely based on the 'Burry Port' 0–6–0 Tank, shown here as a tentative design for the American market. The financial arrangements, however, were never concluded, and so it remained the sole one of its class. When Bassett-Lowke Railways agreed to join the 'Flying Scotsman Tour' to the United States in 1969, it was on the basis that the company had an exclusive concession to produce the souvenir models of No. '4472'. This was in March 1969, but as events proved there was simply not enough time for a static model to be brought to production stage. However, readers might find this very rare picture of the pre-production sample, made at Northampton in 1/72nd scale, of interest. In an effort to fill the gap, a cast lead 'Flying Scotsman' paperweight was hurriedly produced for the company in Eastbourne by the firm of Fernee and Nelson. Once again there was insufficient time, and when the consignment arrived in America for sale on the Tour, the majority of the models had disintegrated under their own weight. Bassett-Lowke at Northampton, however, did produce an extremely nice half-model of No. '4472' which was sold affixed to a wooden commemorative plaque, but a rather nasty LNER transfer let that item down. This whole sorry tale could be entitled 'Beware the Ides of March', or 'How I did not become a Captain of the British Model Train Industry!'.

4 'Across the Mississippi' – 1969 'Flying Scotsman Tour' of the USA enters the Deep South.

4

5

1

1 Sir John Freeman, the then British Ambassador in Washington, visiting the Bassett-Lowke Railways' Exhibition on the 'Flying Scotsman' train during its stop in New York, in October 1969.

3 One of Bassett-Lowke (Railways) Limited versions of a Great Northern 'Single' in electric, with coaches for gauge 1, as catalogued in 1968. These locomotives were originally scheduled for production in Switzerland, but owing to numerous problems, the parts were shipped back to the UK for completion and assembly. The superb paintwork was by Littledale of Brighton. The contract for the coaches to this set was put out to G. Swift of Crowborough, more widely known for his fine model trams.

2 In 1968 Precision Steam Models of London decided to resurrect a late Victorian live steam floor engine design, known as the 'Birmingham Dribbler', and they succeeded in producing a marvellous little brass engine (illustrated) which was every bit as unreliable and dangerous as its forerunner. Regrettably, their sales forecasts were far too optimistic, and the initial production run swamped what might otherwise have become an interesting specialised market. (Track width 2½″.)

2

3

4 One of the few Belgian produced model trains is this Belgian National Railways 'Pacific' for gauge 0, electric, and passenger car by CAM (Chemins de fer Aviation-Marine) of Brussels, *circa 1940*.   Torry Collection

5 Francesco Biaggi (at right) at his trade stand during the Milan Toy Fair, 1965. (See page 168.)

6 The products of Elettren of Italy give us a good insight into how gauge 0 tinplate Märklin trains might have appeared, had they continued to develop that range after the war, as they possess the same quality of being almost a scale model, yet still a creation of fantasy, albeit with great refinement. The 'FS' Pacific illustrated incorporates a great number of metal castings, and one fault in its construction is the tendency of the diecast running board to warp with age. Nonetheless, this was probably one of the loveliest locomotives produced for the post-war period in the pre-war tradition. The original range of Elettren cars, including marvellous tinplate interiors, are still produced today in association with Fulgurex of Lausanne. The 'FS' 2–D–2 electric locomotive illustrated, is one of the first post-war examples of this model by that firm, *circa 1946*. In the late 1960's Elettren produced a range of scale-length CIWL cars, adopting slightly more modern techniques, in particular, the use of plastic roofs. (All Elettren motive power was electric.)

Count Giansanti Collection

1 & 2 A gauge 1 tinplate railway comprising mainly turn of the century lineside features and trains, and a fine N gauge railway of the 1970s. These two scenes underline how fantasy has given way to stark reality over three-quarters of a century.

Gauge 1 layout – Ward Kimball collection and photograph
N gauge layout – Built by M H Cousen, photographed by B Monoghan and reproduced by courtesy of Model Railway Constructor.

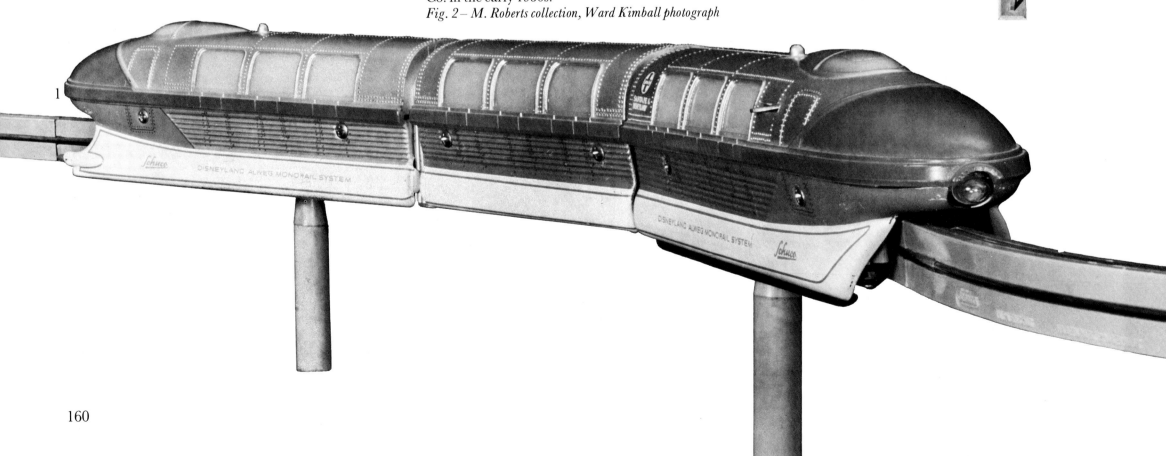

1 Although Schuco of West Germany were not particularly noted for their railway systems, they did produce this interesting monorail (scale 1 : 90), *circa 1965*, based on the 'Disneyland Alweg Monorail' system first introduced at Anaheim in California.

Transport designers have, for many years, experimented with monorail systems. The examples illustrated on this page show how toymakers attempted to follow this trend. Above is Carette's highly sophisticated electric version of the Barmen-Elberfeld Railway as listed in 1905, and at right, a simple and extremely rare clockwork monorail for the American market by Märklin, *circa 1910.* (Car converted from regular gauge 0 range.) Other notable examples were Märklin's hanging monorail system at the turn of the century, and a similar system which was put out by Leland Detroit Manufacturing Co. in the early 1930s.

Fig. 2 – M. Roberts collection, Ward Kimball photograph

3

3 The station buildings pictured here, assembled from Trix 'many ways' units, reflect the bleakness of the immediate post-war era (although the 'many ways' system was actually introduced prior to 1939). Two freelance electric Trix 00 locomotives, an 0–4–0 LNER Tank and an 0–4–0 LMS tender locomotive (both *circa 1950*), go about their various duties. Post-war 'Dinky Toys' adorn the station forecourt.

4

4 Trix-Twin railways were one of the first comprehensive 00 electric systems to be marketed anywhere in the world. History was repeated, in that a proprietor of this company had links with the Bing family and, like his predecessors was greatly encouraged by W. J. Bassett-Lowke.
The close-up illustrations of the pre-war Continental model railway and the panorama of the layout for the British Industries Fair in 1938, show the rapid advances made almost as soon as mass production of 00/H0 ranges became commercially viable.

1 Triang were to be Hornby's main rival for 00 scale trains in post-war Britain, and by commencing a two-rail electric system in the 1950's, they were able to outlast their main rivals, and in fact, Hornby were absorbed by Triang in 1964 (the Triang Empire, cum Hornby, eventually collapsed in the early 1970's). It is not generally considered that Triang's train-producing subsidiary, Rovex, was the principal cause of their problems. Although many of their products were relatively simple by contemporary standards, individual items were excellent and one of the author's favourites is the Great Western 'Lord of the Isles' in 00 scale, electric, *circa 1958*, together with clerestory coaches illustrated here.

2 The three graces – symbols of the stream-line era – were the New York Central 'Hudson' 4–6–4, with the front-end design by Henry Dreyfuss, and alongside the Silver Link and Mallard 'A4' LNER Pacifics, with front-end treatment by Ettore Bugatti. The New York Central 'Hudson' in H0, was introduced by Rivarossi in 1972, and is a further example of the superb design flair of this concern. The two 'A4' Pacifics for 00 electric, *circa 1971*, represent one of the last efforts by Trix in Great Britain.

Liliput of Austria were instrumental in the production of the first batch of Trix 'Flying Scotsmans', and they later provided the chassis for the last Trix British outline range. This picture illustrates the difference in respective scales of H0 – 3.5 millimetres to the foot – and 00 – 4 millimetres to the foot, in that the prototype New York Central locomotive was substantially higher and wider than the LNER locomotives.

3 One of the finest brass locomotives marketed by Fulgurex (this time made in Germany), is this SNCF '141R' introduced in 1974 for gauge 1, in electric. Apart from Märklin's 01 'Pacifics' of the 1930's, Fulgurex is one of the only other firms to offer a similar prototype in H0 (see fig. 4, page 169), gauge 0 (see fig. 3, page 189) and gauge 1. Only 25 examples of the gauge 1 version were produced.

4 H0 electric Rivarossi old and new: An early Rivarossi 'E626' Bo+Bo+Bo, *circa 1950*, and a gold-sprayed 'FS E428, 2+Bo+Bo+2, *circa 1965*. (Observe the detail on the wheel housings.)

Serie speciale per collezionisti

Questo splendido modello è la fedele riproduzione in scala H0 della locomotiva « BAYARD » costruita nelle officine LONGRIDGE & Co. di New Castle nell'anno 1839. E stata la prima locomotiva che ha prestato servizio sulle Ferrovie Italiane ed ha inaugurato il primo tronco ferroviario NAPOLI-PORTICI il 3 Ottobre 1839. Questo modello è interamente costruito in metallo ed è tutto saldato a mano, pezzo per pezzo, con un lavoro paragonabile solo a quello di un maestro giocelliere. Di questo modello per collezionisti ne vengono costruiti solamente 1.000 esemplari, numerati e firmati.

Special series for collectors

This wonderful model is the faithful reproduction, in scale H0, of the « BAYARD » locomotive, built in the LONGRIDGE & Co. workshops in New Castle in the year 1839. It had been the first locomotive which worked on the Italian Railroad and inaugurated the first railway section NAPOLI-PORTICI on October 3rd, 1839. This model is entirely built in metal and is all hand welded, piece for piece, with a work comparable only to that of a master jeweller. Of this collector model they come built only 1.000 exemplaries, numbered and signed.

CARROZZA ANTICA APERTA del 1839
OPEN OLD-TIMER COACH of 1839
Art. SS/02

CARROZZA ANTICA CHIUSA del 1839
CLOSED OLD-TIMER COACH of 1839
Art. SS/03

LOCOMOTIVA ANTICA « BAYARD » del 1839
per sistema 2 rotaie a corrente continua 12 Volts
« BAYARD » OLD-TIMER LOCOMOTIVE of 1839
for 2 rail system - D.C. 12 Volts.
Art. SS/01

5 Pocher of Turin produced some superb plastic H0 rolling stock in the post-war period, but relatively few locomotives. The H0 'Bayard' locomotive for electric running, *circa 1964*, was an example of the supreme Italian art of making patterns for plastic injection dies, and this tradition was to be continued by Rivarossi, who eventually absorbed Pocher's railway products.
By courtesy of Pocher.

1

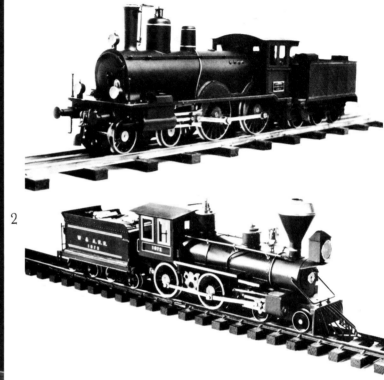

1 The majority of Japanese brass locomotives imported into the United States were for H0 and 0 scales. This magnificent electric model of a 4–6–0 of the Colorado Midland Railway's Pikes Peak Route, represents one of a unique batch of 50 standard gauge ($2\frac{1}{8}''$ gauge), models imported by Wheeler during the 1960's.

2

2 Two examples of the work of Gianini and Mühlethaler of Les Cullayes, Switzerland. Both the American and Swiss locomotives were for live steam, in gauge 0, *circa 1968*. On the untimely death of Gianini in 1969, production was gradually phased out.

3 Walthers were one of the pioneer distributors of model railway products in the United States. Even today their catalogues are eagerly awaited, offering as they do, an enormous range of products. These NYC gauge 0 Pullmans are just one example of made-up cars from standard Walthers' parts, in their current range.

3

4

5

5 W. Hermann of Zurich, who commenced his business in the late 1960's, is probably the most eminent manufacturer of contemporary Swiss railways in gauge 0. The firm's all-metal models were forced to even higher standards to meet the competition from the large manufacturers, who moved into the gauge 0 market in 1969 with excellent plastic products.
By courtesy of Hermann.

4 This SNCF '241 P' locomotive is one of the few examples of Japanese brass products commissioned for a European prototype. Approximately 200 of these electric locomotives were made for Fulgurex in gauge 0, *circa 1968*. Some four years elapsed between the initial order for the locomotives and their delivery. Delays such as this make it difficult to determine the size of batch to be produced at any given time. Most of the Japanese-made European prototypes are pre-sold before delivery and thus they rarely appear on the retail market. The H0 scale Rivarossi electric 'Nord' Pacific, *circa 1972*, together with an 'Armistice' car manufactured by Pocher, *circa 1960*, are also illustrated.

1

1 At about the time of the 1969 Nuremburg Toy Fair, many small, highly specialised manufacturers of 0 gauge appeared. This German Federal Railway 'E91' electric locomotive by Hehr of Stuttgart, utilising component parts by Keiser of Switzerland and Gebauer of Germany, is a typical example of small-batch production for the specialised model trade.
By courtesy of Hehr.

2 A massive 'V200', for gauge 0, by Schieck of Stuttgart. This locomotive required over 4 amps to set it in motion, and had a clutch mechanism which enabled the engine to idle before gradually taking up the transmission. Despite its failings, this 'fuse-buster' really sounded like a diesel.
Circa 1969.
By courtesy of Schieck.

2

Beschreibung meiner V 200 Diesellok, in Spur Null

3 The model railway products of Eastern European countries are relatively rare in the West, and this workmanlike 'CCCP' 4 + 4 + 4 electric locomotive, for gauge 0, has an exceptionally heavy metal cast body, presumably to render it indestructible. Produced by The Moskabel Organisation in Moscow, *circa 1964*, it also forms part of a comprehensive train set which includes very crude tinplate bogie coaches, and pre-wired lineside accessories – of which two examples appear below – not unlike pre-war Lionel.   Count Giansanti Collection

4 One of the first casualties in the gauge 0 rush of 1969 was the 'Pola Maxi' range. The use of plastic, for the working motion may have been a contributory cause of the relative failure in commercial terms of their first series of steam-outline locomotives. As will be observed from the original passenger set illustrated, the mouldings were excellent, and the gauge 0 products of this firm have not been completely discontinued, although there is little sign that the original range is to be extended.

Рис. 8 Блокпост № 1 (дежурит по станции)

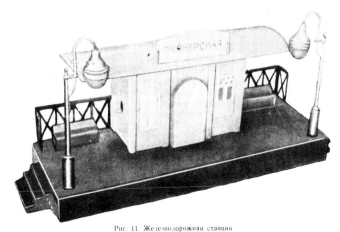

Рис. 11. Железнодорожная станция

1

1 A gauge 1 'Crocodile' locomotive fitted with two electric motors, by Biaggi of Milan. Biaggi commenced manufacturing after 1945 and specialised in small-series production (initially his products were marketed as GEM – Giocattoli Elettro Meccanici). The model illustrated, which was completed in 1970, and is relatively to scale, is in direct line of descent from Märklin's pre-war gauge 1 'short' 'Crocodile' (see fig. 4, page 109). Biaggi produced a particularly fine German 'Pacific', again after the style of Märklin, together with a rather loose interpretation of a BR 'Britannia' Pacific, both for gauge 1. The gauge 1 CIWL car by Wilag also follows Märklin: it was, in fact,

based on the extremely rare 57cm pre-war Märklin series. The H0 diecast electric model of the 'Crocodile', by Märklin, *circa 1949*, has for many years been one of the firm's most expensive H0 locomotives. The 17.5cm Märklin CIWL car in H0 is an early post-war example in tinplate.

2 An early 'TEE' express by Biaggi for 58mm gauge, *circa 1965*.

2

3

3 The pinnacle of the large gauge 'renaissance movement' (0 gauge onwards) has to date been achieved by Wilag of Switzerland, partly in association with Fulgurex. This gas-fired, super-detailed 'S3/6' Maffei Pacific in gauge 1, is probably the finest batch-produced, live-steam model ever to be offered to the European market. The particular item illustrated is, in fact, the prototype of a small super-detailed series, and at the time of photography, it was yet to be fitted with various makers' plates. This locomotive is also produced in a simpler version in both steam and electric, and was first introduced in 1972. A Wilag 'Rheingold' car, *circa 1970*, completes the picture.

4 All brass, Japanese produced, 'SNCF' type '141R' for Fulgurex, *circa 1965*, in H0 electric. The 0 and 1 gauge versions of this locomotive are probably the finest Fulgurex products to date.
By courtesy of Fulgurex

4

Lokomotive SNCF Typ 141-R
Die 141-R-Lokomotiven wurden nach dem letzten Weltkrieg durch die Vereinigten Staaten geliefert. Von keinem anderen Lokomotiventyp besassen die SNCF so viele Einheiten.
Zur vollsten Zufriedenheit wurden sie als Mehrzweck-Lokomotiven in allen Regionen eingesetzt und werden oft als eigentliche Retter der SNCF angesehen. 1340 Einheiten wurden durch die Lokomotivwerke LIMA, ALCO, BALDWIN und MONTREAL-LOKOMOTIVE-WORKS geliefert. Davon 1040 mit Kohlenfeuerung, die restlichen mit Ölfeuerung. 16 Maschinen gingen durch ein Schiffsunglück und eine bei der Landung in Marseille verloren.

Locomotive SNCF Type 141-R
Les 141-R livrées après la dernière guerre par les Etats-Unis constituent le plus grand parc de locomotives du même type construit pour la SNCF.
Elles ont assuré un service mixte sur toutes les régions et donnèrent pleine satisfaction. Elles peuvent être considérées à juste titre comme les sauveurs de la SNCF. 1340 unités furent livrées par les Etablissements LIMA, ALCO, BALDWIN et MONTREAL-LOCOMOTIVE-WORKS dont 1040 chauffées au charbon et les autres au fuel. L'on sait que 16 machines furent perdues dans un naufrage et une lors du débarquement à Marseille.

SNCF Mikado Locomotive, Type 141-R
These historical and numerous locomotives were delivered to France after W.W. II by Messrs. LIMA, ALCO, BALDWIN and MONTREAL-LOCOMOTIVE-WORKS.
1340 units were manufactured (1040 coal-fired and 300 oil-burning). Never before the SNCF received such a big series of the same locomotive type. As a matter of fact, they paid a large tribute to the restoration of the French National Railways. They were affected to the mixed traffic on every regions. 16 engines were unfortunately lost by shipwreck and one fell into the harbour when landing in Marseille.

1

1 The full circle. An assembled static plastic kit model of Stephenson's 'Rocket' in 1/26th scale by Gakken of Japan, *circa 1972*. The firm of Rosebud produced a static plastic kit model of a 'Rocket' in its 'Kitmaster' series, in 00, and Triang produced an electric version in a similar scale.

2 When the Japanese plastic industry turned its attention to the production of model kits, they once again proved their excellence, particularly with their ship, aircraft and motor car kits. Less popular, but still excellent, were a range of locomotives and freight car kits in 1/50th scale by Otaki. This example of one of these kits assembled and weathered, is of a Japanese State Railway 2–8–2 locomotive, affectionately known as the 'Slug', *circa 1971*.

3 An LGB advertisement illustrates how that firm was able to move away from the traditional model train markets. *By courtesy of Lehmann*

Inside the house or out – Summer or Winter – There are no limits to your imagination or the possibilities with LGB equipment

1 This picture might well illustrate a scene in Europe during
   the early 1930's. In fact, the stock comprises a Lehmann
   'Grossbahn' 0–6–2 electric Tank locomotive with a typical
   selection of LGB passenger rolling stock, *circa 1972*. All
   items are modelled on narrow gauge prototypes to gauge
   3 scale for gauge 1 track. The present firm of Lehmann is
   nominally descended from the legendary toy firm of Ernst
   Paul Lehmann, and in 1968, they were the first to lead the
   revival of large-gauge, scale-model trains, utilising mass-
   production through plastic injection moulding techniques.

2 This 'old time' four-wheeled carriage, in plastic, was the only passenger type issued during the relatively short-lived revival of gauge 1 by Märklin. *Circa 1970.*
Official photograph by courtesy of Märklin retouched for Catalogue use

3 I refrain from giving this illustration a title, but it reinforces the suspicion that from the very first, model trains were, in reality, 'not only for the children'.
By courtesy of Fleischmann

4 Fleischmann 20-year anniversary picture, indicating the link with Doll & Cie.
By courtesy of Fleischmann

2

3

4

1 Small-scale railways today have, in many instances, become part of architectural and scenic dioramas. This fact is well illustrated by the Märklin H0 exhibition layout at right.
Photo by courtesy of Märklin.

1

2 An unusual example of freelance design in H0 electric in the form of a three-car diesel unit, reminiscent of the 1930 series of 'Schnell Triebwagen'. This model, designated number '3025' was introduced in 1958 and was produced principally from the components of an H0 freelance American design by Märklin, introduced in 1949, designated Model No. 3017.
Official photograph by courtesy of Märklin retouched for Catalogue use

3 Rowa of West Germany came to prominence as an independent manufacturer around 1967, from which time it produced its own range of trains as well as subcontracting for other model train producers. Notwithstanding the relatively small range of this manufacturer, its products are technically and optically, amongst the finest H0 models ever made. This superb three-car set in H0 electric, known as 'S. Bahn-Triebzug DB Baureihe 420' is a fine example of how far we have travelled since the early days of commercial modelling.

1

1 This panorama of the products of Märklin conveys the
story of miniaturisation over the years. Left to right :-

Gauge 3   'Atlantic'   *circa 1914*
Gauge 1   'Pacific'   *circa 1936*
Gauge 1   'DB' Tank   *circa 1969*

Gauge 0   'Cock O' the North'   *circa 1936*
Minex Narrow gauge Tank,
7mm scale for H0 track   *circa 1970*
H0 'SK 800'   *circa 1939*
Z gauge Mini Club 'Pacific'   *circa 1972*
(*Z gauge train by courtesy of Beatties*)

A GLIMPSE OF FINE SCALE

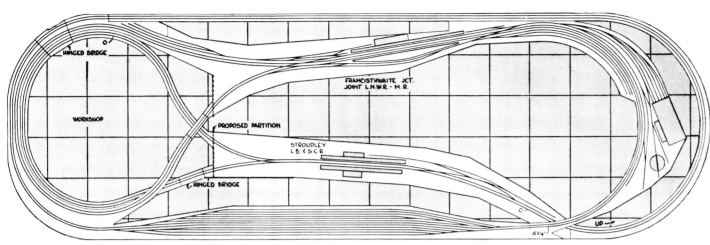

1 Plan drawing of the Norris 'Chilworth' layout.

Much has been written on the subject of the two fine-scale electric 0 gauge railways created by the late W. S. Norris at Byfleet and Chilworth in Surrey, and readers are referred in particular to a series of articles on the 'Norris Railways' which appeared in the 'Model Railway News' editions of June 1957 and February, April and June 1960.

The original layout at Byfleet was based primarily on Great Western Railway practice and existed for some twenty years before being dismantled in 1956. In 1957, a new layout was commenced at Chilworth, though it was never fully completed. It depicted English railways as they operated between 1895 and 1906, and was a fusion of London North Western and Midland workings, with one section operated by the London Brighton and South Coast, together with the South Eastern and Chatham. For good measure some North Eastern stock was also included. In all, 26 locomotives were on shed. The locomotives were built principally by Miller Swan and B. L. Miller. The majority of passenger coaching stock was home-built by W. S. Norris and various associates. Norris's final layout was an attempt to incorporate all the widespread concepts of two-rail, fine-scale modelling in a fully operational model railway, based on prototype practice.

Marcel Darphin's superb 0 gauge, two-rail DC, fine-scale layout at Zug in Switzerland is a continuation of the standards set by Norris, and it also derives its inspiration from the pioneering work of Marescot, the forerunner of Fournereau and Munier in France. This coupled with the experience gained from the work of Gaume, Lequesne, Postel, Houy, Jardel, von Speyr, Girod-Eymery and later Steffen, brought Darphin to the conclusion that 7 millimetres to the foot, 23 millimetres to the metre, i.e. a proportion of $1:43\frac{1}{2}$, was the absolute standard for the construction

A TABLE OF DIMENSIONS FOR GAUGE O, INDICATING THE STANDARDS ADOPTED BY FINE-SCALE MODELLERS AS COMPARED WITH OTHER STANDARDS

(scale $1:43\frac{1}{2}$)	Prototype (mm)	Fine-Scale (mm)	NMRA (mm)	NEM (mm)	Coarse-Scale (mm)	Tinplate (mm)
Wheel thickness	3	3·75	4·44	4·7	5	7
Tyre thickness	2·2	2·75	3·22	3·4	3·5	5
Flange thickness	0·8	1	1·21	1·3	1·5	2
Flange height	0·8	1·25	1·14	1·5/2·1	1·5	3
Radius – flange/tyre	0·3	0·5	0·63	0·5	0·5	0·5
Tread cone	4°	3°	3°	3°	3°	3°
Flange taper	7°	10°	—	inside 20° outside 10°	—	inside only
Protrusion of wheel boss (inside boxes)		0·5	—	0·5	0·5	2
Back-to-back	29·8	29	28·39	28·4	28	26·75
Inside flange to outside opposite flange		30	29·76	29·8	29·5	
Minimum clearance flangeways		1·75	2·1	2·1	2·5	3
(recommended increase to 2·25 on curves under 1200 mm)						
Outside checkrail to inside opposite running-rail – minimum		30	30·37	30	29·5	29
Outside of checkrail to outside of wing-rail – maximum		28·5	28·27	27·9	27	26
RECOMMENDATIONS FOR BUFFER-TO-BUFFER OPERATION:						
Distance between two parallel main-tracks		100 mm				
Minimum frog angle		1:8				
Minimum radius on mainline, continuous curves		2250 mm				
Minimum radius on mainline, opposing curves (crossovers)		3250 mm				

of his model railway system. These proportions were the fine-scale standards established by the Model Railway Club of Great Britain before the first world war, subsequently endorsed by J. N. Maskelyne and brought to commercial reality by Marescot in the 1920's. Thus, car by car, track by track, the Zug layout – first conceived in 1948 – was commenced.

Fine-scale wheel flanges required unorthodox techniques for rolling stock suspension, and track-work required a certain flexibility, as it does in reality. These needs, and those of others working in this field, led to the establishment – by Marcel Darphin – of 'Darstaed', a firm formed to supply these specialist requirements by way of a small output of models and component parts. In this work, Marcel Rossi of Paris (Darphin's lifelong friend) has been instrumental in providing prototypes for freight cars and also most of the superb passenger cars that appear on the layout. The layout was first built in H0 Märklin track in order to prove operational movements. After many years of further study and construction, a train ran over the first loop in 1967. The layout, still under construction, is housed in an area 12 metres long and 7 metres wide. At various stages, Marcel Darphin was assisted by Heinz Huber, and the construction of the scenery has been the particular province of Kurt Drescher and Susi Darphin. Leaving aside arguments concerned with the mathematical accuracy of one scale as opposed to another, one of the minimum standards set by fine-scale modellers was that all their measurements should lead to a high degree of optical reality, and long trains using scale couplings, must be seen to run buffer-to-buffer in much the same way as in normal railway practice.

2

2 'The Works: from left to right, SNCF '231 D' former 'Etat' by Lequesne, '231G' by Gaume, and, foreground right, '231E' by Delienne. (The control panel is a temporary arrangement, and does not reflect the builder's final intention.)

1   2   3

6   7   8

1 SECR 'Stirling' 'F' Class and train passing under bridge on approach to Stroudley Station. Locomotive by Miller, coaching stock by Norris and associates.

6 'Precursor' Tank No. 44 on LNWR train passing through Francisthwaite Station. Locomotive completed by Miller from an original model by A. P. Dowley; coaching stock by A. Cowan, Norris, Miller and Associates. *(Photo A. P. Dowley)*

2 Francisthwaite station (LNWR/MR joint), so named after Francis Webb of the LNWR and Samuel Waite Johnson of the Midland Railway.

3 LBSC Railway 'Southbourne' express train passing site of the LNWR/MR Station. Locomotive by Miller, coaching stock by Norris and associates.

7 LNWR 'Precursor' Tank No. 44 on typical LNWR train approaching Stroudley Station.

4

5

9

10

4 'Johnson' 2–4–0 on MR, local train climbing bank at rear of Francisthwaite Station. Locomotive by Miller, coaching stock by Norris and associates.

8 Perspective of trackwork in progress. Each section of track was assembled on a plywood base, cut to fit its location. Units were laid on sponge rubber carpet underlay to facilitate levelling and super-elevation. (Baseboard constructed of $\frac{5}{8}''$ blockboard).

5 LNWR No. 1988 'Hurricane' of the 'Experiment' Class 4–6–0, by Miller Swan, heads a train passing LNWR locomotive shed area showing a water tower by L. Ward.

9 'Bessemer' of the LBSCR 'B2' Class. Built and painted by Miller. It was, in fact, the last locomotive to be put into service before the layout's demise in 1965.

10 LNWR brake van by J. P. Richards.

1

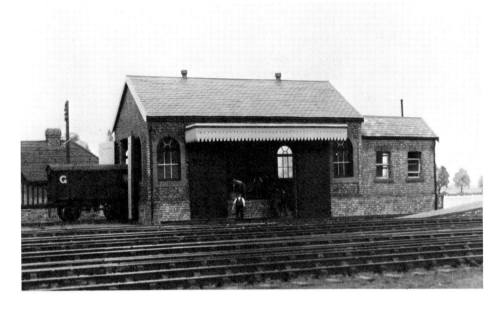

2

3

4

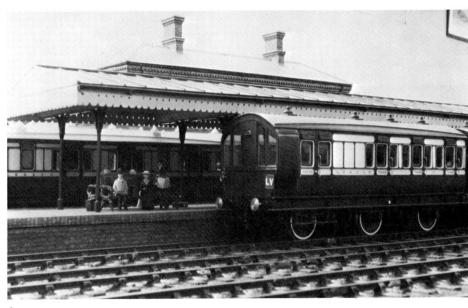

1 & 2 Two views of Francisthwaite Goods Shed, illustrating the
outstanding quality of the lineside features on the Norris
railway.

4 LBSC express train on main line, with set of 'balloon'
carriages in bay at Stroudley Station. Coaching stock by
Norris and associates.
All Norris layout photos – V. Reader Collection

3 Francisthwaite West Signal Box for LNWR section.

5

5 An example of an ex-Norris locomotive in foreign fields is this model of a 'Midland' 4–4–0 by Evans/Miller. It is double-headed with a Midland 'Single', detailed and refurbished by V. Reader from an original model built by W. Cox. The Midland clerestory partially showing is by Exley.   Midland 'Single': Singer Collection

6

6 This LBSCR 'Plumpton', formerly one of the Norris locomotives, was completed by B. L. Miller from an original model by J. N. Maskelyne. LBSCR coaches by Archangel Models. The diminutive 'Terrier' Tank of unknown make was repainted by Littledale of Brighton.

1 A man and his trains.

2 Leaving Royville West.

3 Western entry to Royville. Locomotive exchange section.

4 Rivarossi DB 0–6–0 Tank, with freight car by Hamann, trundles over main road to Royville.

5 'P8' by Gebauer crossing Royville West. Super-detailed DB freight car by Pfannmüller.

1 SNCF '241P' enters Royville, and the world of model
railways almost merges with reality.

2 'Train Bleu' at Royville, CIWL cars by Rossi.

1   Darstaed BLS 'Ae 4/4' on Swiss section, going on to Spiez with a freight train made up of Darstaed cars. (Overhead catenary is scheduled for the final phase of construction.)

2   On shed at Royville: at right, 'CC 7100' by Baveret, at left, '231 G' PLM Pacific by Gaume.

3   At Royville shed: at left, a '141 R' by Fulgurex, at right, 'CC 2100' by Fulgurex (modified to fine-scale).

1   Morning arrival at Royville West.

2   'Day's End' – The 'Golden Arrow', illustrating Darstaed
    'Inox' cars, rushes by, while farm labourers end their toil.
    Photo Steffen.

Beeson's bench.

THE GENIUS OF BEESON

Had James Stanley Beeson decided to become a jeweller instead of a model train maker, he may well have been a latter-day Fabergé. It is seldom that a person's surname becomes synonymous with the absolute refinement of a particular art. At the risk of labouring the point. Beeson is to model trains as the names of Messrs. Rolls and Royce are to motor cars, and superlatives must end there.

Connoisseurs among the post-war generation (who, unlike their predecessors, had little experience of an era abounding with craftsmen) were the first to appreciate the true significance of the work of this remarkable artist/engineer. A Beeson model locomotive, judged in creative terms, is simply an extremely fine object; as an interpretation of one of the most emotive pieces of machinery in the history of mankind, it is almost definitive.

Such criticism as exists of Beeson's work focuses upon the fact that his locomotives are too pristine, that they do not illustrate the imperfections of the prototypes. Criticism of this nature, however valid, can be sustained with equanimity.

I hope at some future date to deal with the work and times of James Stanley Beeson in a separate volume, but suffice it to say that since 1924 when he set up in business on his own account, he has produced over 1,500 locomotives, mainly for 0 gauge (7mm scale). In Beeson's own view, his work from the 1960's onwards is the most important, and his finest model is always the one he is about to complete.

Our passing glance at Beeson's model locomotives does not concentrate on the most glamorous or upon his latest work. It is rather an attempt to illustrate a typical cross-section of his models commencing with one of the first locomotives built for G. P. Keen's legendary 'Pantry Dockyard Railway'.

In order to avoid undue handling of the Beeson locomotives, it was necessary, in certain instances, to photograph models *in situ* on their display bases. In those instances retaining bolts may be visible between the wheels.

All locomotives illustrated in this section are for electric operation, in 0 gauge unless otherwise specified.

1 'Early days', depicting (despite the poor quality of this photograph) the first of a batch of three Dean 'Singles' commenced in 1929, the last of which was delivered in 1947. (Tinplate construction for three-rail, coarse-scale.)
Photo J. S. Beeson Collection

2 One of a pair of North London Tanks delivered to G. P. Keen for his 'Pantry Dockyard Railway'. This particular locomotive was finished in 1923 while Beeson was still employed with a London firm of estate agents. In all, six of these little Tank locomotives were completed in tinplate, during those early years (three-rail, coarse-scale).
Photo J. S. Beeson Collection

3 Introduction to catalogue – price list, for 1932 catalogue.

7 m/m Scale Model, L.N.E.R. "Pacific."

Models for Advertising and Film Purposes.

JAMES S. BEESON,
147 NEASDEN LANE,
LONDON, N.W.10.

Telephone: Gladstone 2156.

INTRODUCTION.

For a number of years past Beeson products have enjoyed a world wide reputation as being the most characteristic and near to scale obtainable.

The high standard maintained is due to extreme concentration on every detail. Before construction photographs and drawings of each part are studied with the utmost care, the result giving individuality and technique unsurpassed.

To the constructor, Beeson fittings are invaluable.

Mechanisms are a speciality. Designed to show maximum daylight under the boiler, they are separately built to fit any locomotive. Complete chassis can be supplied with or without valve gear that is exact in every detail.

A comprehensive selection of name and number plates is kept in stock, and orders for new ones are promptly executed.

Chimneys, domes, etc., are individually turned with the aid of photographs to give the correct atmosphere.

Blue prints are produced with a very thin and clear line to facilitate accurate measurement.

All other fittings marketed bear the same degree of quality and finish that means so much in the eyes of the connoisseur.

Prices of Beeson Locomotives.

Gauge "O" (Add 25% extra on List price for Gauge "1.")

Type.	Super detail. £ s. d.	Cheaper Model. £ s. d.	Electric or Spring movement.	Minimum Curve. diameter.
L.M.S.				
Royal Scot or Baby Scot	52 10 0	35 0 0	either	7 ft.
Compound or Re-built Claughton	45 10 0	30 0 0	„	7 ft.
2-6-4 or 2-6-2 tanks	45 0 0	26 0 0	„	6 ft.
5900 Class, or Class "2" 4-4-0	35 10 0	26 0 0	„	6 ft.
Standard 0-6-0 tender goods	35 0 0	19 10 0	„	6 ft.
0-6-0 tank	32 0 0	17 10 0	„	6 ft.
Mogul	52 0 0	35 0 0	„	6 ft.
0-6-0 or 0-4-0 dockyard tank	32 0 0	21 0 0	electric only	6 ft.
Garratt. 2-6-0 0-6-2	700 0 0	95 0 0	either	10 ft.
L.N.W.R. Section.				
0-8-0 goods	35 0 0	26 0 0	„	6 ft.
Prince of Wales 4-6-0	35 0 0	26 0 0	„	6 ft.
Webbs 0-6-2 coal engine or "Watford" tank	25 0 0	15 0 0	electric only	6 ft.
0-6-0 tender coal engine	32 0 0	19 10 0	„	6 ft.
L.N.E.R.				
Pacific or Mikado	50 10 0	37 0 0	either	8 ft.
Sandringham, Shire, or Mogul	45 0 0	30 0 0	„	7 ft.
2-6-4 tank	40 0 0	25 0 0	„	8 ft.
0-6-0 J.39 class	35 0 0	19 10 0	„	6 ft.
Garratt	220 0 0	110 0 0	„	10 ft.
G.C.R. section.				
Atlantic or 4-6-0 types	35 0 0	26 0 0	„	7 ft.
"Director" or 4-6-2- tank	35 0 0	25 0 0	„	7 ft.
G.N.R. section.				
Atlantic 1430 or 990 class	35 0 0	25 0 0	electric only	7 ft.
0-6-2T or Saddle tank	30 0 0	17 0 0	„	6 ft.
Stirling. 8 ft. single	35 0 0	25 0 0	„	8 ft.
7 ft 6 in. single	30 0 0	20 0 0	„	8 ft.
0-4-4 tank	50 0 0	25 0 0	„	6 ft. 6 in.
0-6-0 and 0-4-2 tender locos.	31 0 0	18 0 0	„	6 ft.
Ivate Single 4-2-2	35 0 0	19 10 0	„	6 ft.
N.E.R. Section.				
4-4-0 inside cylinder	35 0 0	19 0 0	„	6 ft.
4-4-0 outside	40 0 0	26 0 0	electric only	6 ft.
Atlantic	42 0 0	30 0 0	either	8 ft.
4-8-0 or 4-6-2 tanks	35 0 0	23 0 0	„	8 ft.
N.B.R. Atlantic	32 0 0	19 15 0	„	8 ft.
G.W.R.				
King Class	55 0 0	35 0 0	either	8 ft.
Hall, Castle, Star, or Saint	45 0 0	30 0 0	„	6 ft.
2-6-2 or 2-8-0 tanks	35 0 0	25 0 0	„	6 ft.
2-4-0 or 0-4-2 tanks	24 0 0	18 0 0	electric only	6 ft.
Pannier Tanks	28 10 0	18 0 0	„	6 ft.
4-4-0 outside crank locos.	37 0 0	25 0 0	„	6 ft.
Aberdare 2-6-0	33 0 0	19 15 0	„	6 ft.
0-6-0 goods	27 0 0	18 0 0	„	6 ft.
SOUTHERN.				
"Lord Nelson"	55 0 0	37 0 0	either	8 ft.
King Arthur or 4-6-0 goods	38 0 0	23 0 0	„	6 ft.
Schools or Mogul	40 0 0	26 0 0	„	6 ft.
4-8-0 or 4-6-2 tanks	40 0 0	26 0 0	„	8 ft.
4-4-0 tender locos	35 0 0	21 0 0	„	8 ft.
Drummond 0-4-4 tank	27 0 0	18 0 0	electric only	6 ft.
0-6-0 tender goods	30 0 0	19 10 0	„	6 ft.
L.B. & S.C.R. section.				
Atlantic or Mogul	37 0 0	25 0 0	either	8 ft.
Billington 4-4-0	37 0 0	25 0 0	electric only	8 ft.

Quotation for any type of loco, for any scale up to 1½ inch to the foot sent on receipt of particulars.

4

5

6

5&6 Beeson created seventeen models of the Stanier 'Duchess' Class Pacific, ranging from basic coarse-scale examples, to super-detailed models, with full inside-cylinder motion. Illustrated in figs 5 and 6 is a 'Duchess of Montrose' completed during 1952 in nickel silver for fine-scale running. This is one of the last examples of this type of locomotive delivered by Beeson. Detail of a further LMS model is illustrated in fig. 4. This tinplate model of a 'Patriot' Class locomotive, was originally built in 1928 as one of a large batch, a considerable number of which were marketed under other trade names. The backhead fittings were part of a complete re-build and restoration carried out by the maker in 1971.

1 A refurbished model of a 'Sandringham' in tinplate, for three-rail running to coarse-scale standards, *circa 1936*, one of a batch of twelve.

2 LNER 'VI' Tank, *circa 1938*, to coarse-scale standards, completely refurbished and part of an original batch of twelve. It must be remembered that not all models laid down in batches were sold direct by J. S. Beeson, and firms such as Walkers and Holtzapffel, Bassett-Lowke, Edward Exley, Milbro and Premier Models, marketed Beeson-made products to special order under their own labels.

3

3 'J39' of tinplate construction, coarse-scale, *circa 1939*. Numerous examples of this particular type were made primarily for sale through the maker's trade customers. This model retailed at £11.00 during that time. (Refurbished 1971).

4 This superb model of an LNER 'A3' Pacific 'Robert the Devil' clearly illustrates the supremacy of this builder, even in the embryo days of scale modelling. This particular model was one of a batch of six made between 1936 and 1940, (refurbished 1971 to fine-scale standards), although an earlier example was supplied to Kodak's in 1928 for use in their cine research department.

4

2

1 There is little doubt that in terms of commissions, models of Great Western locomotives were the most numerous. This model of 'King Richard I' was one of a batch of six made between 1945 and 1947 for two-rail to fine-scale standards. It was also one of the first nickel silver models, *circa 1947*.

2 Backhead of 'King Richard I' displaying standard three-dimensional Beeson fittings. These fittings, together with many other components – wheels, axle boxes, valve gear, etc. – were available as separate items.

1 A one-off example of a 'Stirling Single' in H0 scale for three-rail operation, constructed in nickel silver, *circa 1956*. Beeson produced relatively few models for H0 scale.

2 Detail of outside frame motion of 'Bulldog'. See fig. 1, page 204.

3

3 This London North Western 'Saddle Tank' for fine-scale, was in the maker's opinion the most difficult small Tank engine to model. Six were made between 1959 and 1962, of which four were in the form illustrated, and two retained only the spectacle-plate part of the cab.

2 Only two super-detailed, fine-scale models of this Great Western 0–4–2 Motor Tank were built, *circa 1956*. In fig. 1 the locomotive is depicted with a Great Western coach by A. H. Pealing, one of the most prolific builders of high quality coaching stock.

3   This fine-scale model of Webb's first rebuild of
    Ramsbottom's 'Lady of the Lake' Class was the last model
    of a batch of five built between 1959 and 1962.

3

1 Here we take a many-sided view of one of the latest models illustrated in this section, the Churchward rebuild of Dean's famous 'Bulldog' Great Western Express locomotive 'Madras', *circa 1958*. This particular model was one of a pair, the other model having the motor in the tender to allow the fitting of full inside motion between the frames.

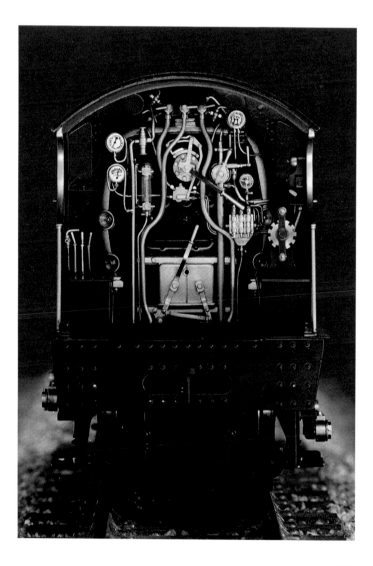

1 Our brief stay in the esoteric world of James Stanley
   Beeson concludes with a view of one of his little Collett
   Great Western 'Pannier' Tanks, built in 1946, at work on
   the Marcel Darphin layout in Switzerland.

BIBLIOGRAPHY

The following books are those which I, personally, have found extremely useful. The list is by no means comprehensive, but is simply a guide for readers who may wish to gain further insights into this diverse subject.

MODEL ELECTRIC LOCOMOTIVES AND RAILWAYS
Henry Greenly   Cassell & Co. Ltd. 1922
One of the rare insights into the thinking of this remarkable engineer as it related to the electrification of model locomotives, both in electric and steam outline. It is a great pity that so little of the background to this man's work with the German manufacturers has been recorded.

DIE MODELLEISENBAHN
(No English Edition)   Union Deutsche
G. Reder   Verlagsgesellschaft 1926
Concerned wholly with the working and management of model railways, this was one of the few books published on the Continent to deal with this aspect of railway modelling, utilising in the main proprietary models and accessories.

RIDING THE TINPLATE RAILS
         Model Craftsman
Louis H. Hertz   Publishing Corp. 1944
One of the first books to take a serious look at the history of model trains, and also one of the most readable 'text books' on the subject. Although written from an American point of view, it includes some interesting insights into the Hornby era on both sides of the Atlantic.

FIFTY YEARS OF MODEL MAKING
G. Holland   Bassett-Lowke Ltd. 1949
A very valuable 'in house' review of the history of Bassett-Lowke Limited from the turn of the century, although it commences with a startling chronological error concerning the introduction of 'The Lady of The Lake' and 'Black Prince' locomotives.

MESSRS. IVES OF BRIDGEPORT
Louis H. Hertz   Mark Haber & Co. 1950
One of the few definitive histories of a model train manufacturer. The loss of so much original material has proved a great obstacle in enlarging this highly specialised body of literature.

COLLECTING MODEL TRAINS
Louis H. Hertz   Mark Haber & Co. 1956
This is really the definitive book about collecting model trains. Once again it is written from a primarily American standpoint, and nothing remotely as good as this, dealing with the European scene, was to appear until Gustav Reder's classic work some thirteen years later.

MODEL RAILWAYS 1838–1939
        George Allen
Hamilton Ellis   & Unwin Ltd. 1962
The first treatise on the historical aspect of model railways to be published in England. Written in a highly personalised style (where memory and fact do not always coincide) it is nonetheless an extremely useful reference work, and includes an excellent selection of photographs.

THE TRAINS OF LIONEL'S STANDARD GAUGE ERA
        Railroad Model
Harold H. Carstens Craftsman 1964
An excellent review of Lionel's most glamorous products.

THE COLLECTOR'S BOOK OF THE LOCOMOTIVE
Edwin P. Alexander Clarkson N. Potter Inc. 1966
A pot-pourri of 'railwayana'. The sections dealing with model trains are excellent.

THE GOLDEN AGE OF TOYS
Jac Remise & Jean Fondin Edita Lausanne 1967
Although not primarily a book on model trains, it is nonetheless a classic book in that it explores the visual possibilities of portraying toys. The toys, including railways, are principally of the pre-1914 era.

THE TOY COLLECTOR
Louis H. Hertz   Funk & Wagnalls 1969
Louis H. Hertz returns in this book to discuss the techniques and philosophy of toy collecting in general, although a great many of the illustrations are of relatively early American trains.

MODEL RAILWAY ENGINES
J. E. Minns   Weidenfeld & Nicolson 1969
This book is particularly strong on the history of early English and French brass steam locomotives. It is also an excellent guide to the history of miniature passenger-hauling railways, and includes some memorable contemporary photographs.

MIT UHRWERK DAMPF & STROM
        Alba Buchverlag 1969
CLOCKWORK STEAM AND ELECTRIC
(English Edition)   Ian Allan Ltd. 1972
Gustav Reder
Undoubtedly the most comprehensive review of the subject to date, including an extremely useful section which provides brief histories of principal manufacturers.

MODEL TRAINS
Uberto Tosco   Igda, Novara 1969
Introduction to English Edition
Gerald Pollinger   Orbis Books 1972
Although this publication is primarily concerned with illustrations of post-war H0 and 00 model trains, the introduction to the English edition includes one of the most comprehensive comparative tables relating to the history of gauge and scale.

AUF KLEINEN SPUREN (No English Edition)
Udo Becher   Transpress 1970
One of the few books on the subject to come out of East Germany. It devotes a great deal of space to makers virtually unknown to collectors in the West.

OLDER LOCOMOTIVES 1900–1942
P. G. Gomm   Nelson 1970
A small but interesting review of the less exotic locomotives, mainly for gauge 0. Almost all the items illustrated are British prototypes.

RECENT LOCOMOTIVES 1947–1970
P. E. Randall   Nelson 1970
A companion to the above, it has a particularly good review of the last post-war Hornby gauge 0 locomotives.

THE WORLD OF MODEL TRAINS
Guy R. Williams   Andre Deutsch 1970
This book does not concentrate on the world of commercial model railways, but rather attempts to cover all facets of the subject, including layout construction, garden railways, etc. The book includes several memorable photographs.

TOY TRAINS OF YESTERYEAR
Case Kowal Model Craftsman Publishing Corp. 1972
An excellent compendium of articles written by Case Kowal for 'Toy Trains Magazine' in 1953/54. This publication is typical of the in-depth information that at most times has been available to American collectors.

WORLD LOCOMOTIVE MODELS

George Dow   Adams & Dart   1973

Mr. Dow has chosen a rather unusual approach by presenting the international development of prototype steam, diesel and electric locomotives through examples of exhibition models. The prototype information contained in this book is far more comprehensive than the background to the models and their respective makers.

CATALOGUE REPRODUCTIONS

Although the reproduction of individual catalogues has been widely practised in America and the Continent for some time, compendia of old catalogues published in book form are a recent innovation. In view of the scarcity of original material, a list of publications that I have found most useful is given below :-

BASSETT-LOWKE RAILWAYS

     Bassett-Lowke

A. L. Levy   (Railways) Limited   1968

A trade catalogue including catalogue reproductions of the original Bassett-Lowke company – 1902–1963.

DIE WEITEN SPUREN

Claude Jeanmaire   Verlag Eisenbahn   1969

A volume of reprinted Märklin catalogues.

GEBRÜDER BING – 1902   Mogens Wind   1971

A reprinted dealers catalogue (inc. ships, stationary engines, cars etc.).

BING, DIE MODELLBAHNEN UNSERER GROSSVÄTER

Claude Jeanmaire   Verlag Eisenbahn   1972

A volume of reprinted Bing catalogues.

ERNST PLANK

Jan Blenken, Rolf Richter & Reinhard Rossig

     Weinheimer

     Auktionshaus   1973

A reprinted dealers catalogue (inc. ships, stationary engines, cars etc.).

HORNBY BOOK OF TRAINS

F. R. Gorham   Oxford Publishing Co.   1973

A reprint of Hornby catalogues for 1927–32.

THE STORY OF GAUGE 0 HORNBY TRAINS

Peter Randall   The Cranbourn Press Ltd.   1974

Reprinted illustrations from Meccano Magazines 1922–39.

DIE ANDEREN NÜRNBERGER

Carlernst Baecker & Dieter Haas

     Hobby Haas   1974

Band 1 – Karl Bub, Joh. Distler KG, Georges Carette & Cie., Doll & Cie.

Band 2 – J. Falk, Gebrüder Fleischmann, Ernst Paul Lehmann, (SG) Günthermann, Jos. Kraus & Co.

Band 3 – Johann And. Issmayer, Ernst Plank, Tipp & Co., Georg Levy.

Reprints of single catalogues in respect of the above makers. (Includes various lines.)

In addition to the above, readers are particularly recommended to a periodical that appeared monthly between 1909 and 1918 entitled 'Models, Railways and Locomotives', edited by Henry Greenly. These publications are particularly important in that they cover a vital period during which, apart from trade catalogues and various editions of Bassett-Lowke's 'Model Railway Handbook', little contemporary published information on European scenic model railways is available. In addition to this material, the trade periodicals that have appeared since the 1920's provide an invaluable running history of model railways in all their forms.

EXPLANATORY NOTES

1   In order to avoid repetition, where an item was produced exclusively for Bassett-Lowke by one of the German manufacturers, a note indicating *for Bassett-Lowke* will appear beneath the caption.

2   In cases where trains were not primarily produced to run on track, their wheel track width has been noted in order to give some indication of their relative size.

3   Collection credits have been given only when requested by their owners, and then in the style designated by them.

4   A great deal of research has been carried out in order to give the most accurate indication possible of the dates of the various items (in most instances, this is the date of introduction). It must be remembered that catalogues, while an excellent source of information, can be misleading in this context, and every care has been taken to corroborate dates with whatever contemporary information has been available.

Produced and created by
NEW CAVENDISH BOOKS